the
magic

the magic feather

The Truth About "Special Education"

LORI GRANGER AND BILL GRANGER

E. P. DUTTON   NEW YORK

This is for Ginny Olmstead

Published in the United States by E.P. Dutton,
a division of New American Library,
2 Park Avenue, New York, N.Y. 10016.

Library of Congress Cataloging-in-Publication Data

Granger, Lori.
  The magic feather.

  Bibliography: p.
  Includes index.
1. Exceptional children—Education—United States.
2. Exceptional children—United States—Rating of—
Evaluation. I. Granger, Bill. II. Title.
LC3981.G73   1986   371.9'0973   86-8973
ISBN: 0-525-24451-4

Published simultaneously in Canada by Fitzhenry & Whiteside, Ltd., Toronto

COBE

DESIGNED BY EARL TIDWELL

10 9 8 7 6 5 4 3 2 1
First Edition

It is not possible, I think, to imagine a more contemptible proceeding than to confront a child with a set of puzzles, and after an hour's monkeying with them, proclaim to the child, or to his parents, that here is a C-minus individual. It would not only be a contemptible thing to do. It would be a crazy thing to do. . . .

—WALTER LIPPMANN

If there is anything that we wish to change in the child, we should first examine it and see whether it is not something that could better be changed in ourselves.

—CARL GUSTAV JUNG

Contents

Introduction

Each year, in school conference rooms across the country, the parents of more than 1 million schoolchildren receive this grim news: Your child is "mildly handicapped"—learning-disabled, mildly retarded, or emotionally disturbed.

The usual course is to suggest special programs to teach the child "skills," though the implication of the handicapped label is that the child will never be normal. He must be removed from regular classes either full time or part time. He cannot function without expert help.

Often the schools offer to help the parents with their "grieving process" in learning to think of their child as handicapped.

In 1982 this happened to us. We did not believe it. We fought the diagnosis. We won—though we had to leave the public school system to do it.

Since then we have studied the ways children are labeled and treated in our schools—children who are successful outside school, whose "problems" are entirely school-based.

We have learned some startling things. We have found that the process that pins such labels on children is at best expedient and at worst outright fraud.

We learned that there is no accepted body of scientific knowledge that has found the causes of school-based problems—or agrees on the cures. There is only constant experimentation in the classroom, using children as guinea pigs. When educators say their conclusions about a child are based on known scientific findings, they are lying. It is just that simple.

No one knows what a "learning-disabled" child is, and the difference between him and another called "emotionally disturbed" or "retarded" may be nonexistent. What they share is that they did not "fit in" in a regular classroom. Their teachers did not like them. It is just that simple.

A proper scientific theory must be subject to disproof, in the philosopher Karl Popper's dictum. The speculations that lie at the heart of Special Education are not scientific, for they are of such a vague and accusatory character that they can never be disproved.

A parent who is told his child is learning-disabled can never prove that he is not, because any child who does not please his teacher can be called learning-disabled. The same thing is true for the supposed hyperactives and emotionally disturbed children.

Since children are called retarded on the basis of their IQ scores, a new score on a new test can prove them nonretarded; but in every case we've known where that has happened—and many parents have written of such occurrences—the educators have merely shifted ground and called the child something else.

In speaking out about this, we have faced a great deal

of criticism. Are we maintaining that there is no such thing as a handicapped child? Shouldn't there be special provisions made for children in wheelchairs? Do we really believe there are no autistic or severely retarded children? Are we suggesting deaf children should not be educated?

This criticism is a smoke screen. Of course there are handicapped children, and no one should deny them the special provisions that make education possible for them. But do we help handicapped kids by isolating them? Do we help ourselves? And is school segregation—and that is what Special Education comes down to, even to the nasty reality that it is sometimes used to promote racial segregation—a good thing for any child?

Children who are successful in every sphere of life except the school are not handicapped, and educators are flimflamming when they pretend that they are. These are the children whom educators, who feel they can make words mean what they want them to mean, call "mildly handicapped." Their resemblance to children with genuine medical problems is fabricated; their supposed difference from "normal" children is wildly exaggerated.

To treat a child who has trouble following directions or is too active in a classroom as a medical case is dishonest and robs the genuinely handicapped of funds and services they need to deal with their very real problems.

National surveys show that teachers identify nearly 60 percent of their students as needing special or remedial help. The trend is to locate the blame for this mismatch of students' needs with the regular school program inside the students' heads—it is a consistent finding in several recent surveys that teachers identify a little over 20 percent of their students as being handicapped and in need of Special Education.[1]

There is something wrong with a system that increasingly justifies its growing failure rate by calling more and more children mentally defective. Such a trend sooner or later calls into question the legitimacy of our schools.

Nearly one out of every eight kids in school are in Special Education today—about four times the number that would be in such programs if they were limited to children with genuine medical handicaps. This is too many and educators know it. It is a national disgrace, and a personal tragedy for thousands of parents and children.

Too many parents have been willing to be conned into playing the labels game. Happy to find their child called "perceptually impaired" rather than "retarded," they have been unwilling to question what the label really means.

This book is not about what is wrong with Special Education. It is about what is wrong with education as a whole. The labeling and the sham treatments are not bad only for those children caught in the Special Ed trap.

Every time a child is called mentally defective and sent off to the special class for some trivial defect, the children who are left in the regular classroom receive a message: No one is above suspicion; everyone is being watched by the authorities; nonconformity is dangerous.

When this happens, the range of normality becomes a little narrower. The classroom becomes a little duller and more oppressive. And the chance that true learning will take place there becomes that much less.

This is not only a book of criticism but a book of education for parents about what this thing called Special Education is really all about. It is also a book of sharing the experiences of parents who faced real problems with the schools and their kids. It is also a resource book for parents to show them how to fight the mislabeling of their children, how to really help their children overcome school problems, and how to ensure a future full of great expectations for them, instead of certain failure.

PART ONE

Alec's Song

1

Premonitions

When Alec was four and in a Montessori-method preschool, we were told that children preparing to go to public school kindergarten the following fall could take part in a screening program. It was said that simply and that innocently. We took Alec to the public school on the day the program was held. This was the beginning of our nightmare, one that lasted three years.

We overcame the nightmare. This first part of the book is to tell what happened to Alec and to us so that the rest of the book—explaining the problems in Special Education and in misdiagnosis of children with special learning problems and how parents can overcome their own education nightmares—will make you understand two things.

First, there are terrible things happening in Special Education. Children are labeled with learning disabilities that don't exist, while other learning problems are ignored. The labeling of children in education is an epidemic affecting some 12 percent of all children in public education. To escape the mislabeling problem, thousands of parents abandon public education only to find the problem exists in the private schools as well.

Second, strong parents—and concerned teachers— willing to fight a well-intended system that has become a monster can slay the monster. But they have to be armed with a complete guide to Special Education—what it is and what it isn't, what all the terms mean (and where the terms, some of them preposterous, came from), and what parents and concerned teachers can do to help children get the education they deserve and avoid a system intent on teaching children how to be failures.

It is difficult for us to tell our story, even now. But the abuses of Special Education and misdiagnosis thrive in silence.

This is what happened to us: white, suburban, middle-class parents and a nice, average little boy who did some things better than other kids his age and some things worse. It is happening to Alecs and Alices all over the country every single day.

We live in a suburb of Chicago. We are writers and editors who grew up in the city. Bill went to Catholic schools and Lori went to public schools. When it began, we lived in a suburb so average it always seems to fall into the exact middle of any Chicago area survey of income, home values, and taxes. Because we grew up in the city and thought we had "street smarts," our guard was down when it came to dealing with the local public school. After all, this was suburbia, where people run to to escape the problems of the city, including Chicago's notoriously bad public school system.

On the day of the screening for kindergarten, Lori took Alec to the local public school. The room was full of four-year-olds staring at other four-year-olds in the charming way of children suddenly realizing there are lots of other children in the world.

Alec was our only child. He had stubborn brown hair, cloudless blue eyes, and a perpetual smile. He was a child without a history of childhood illnesses. He was much loved.

The man who was screening Alec was called a psychologist. We would discover that the title *psychologist* is very loosely applied in most schools. It can refer to anyone with a master's degree in psychology, which means anyone who has gone to college for five years instead of four, and it is a term that ordinary parents can find as solemn and intimidating as the word *doctor*.

At the prescreening, the psychologist—who had a master's degree—said he was testing Alec's skill levels. This was not true. He said he was not testing Alec's intelligence level. And this was not true. The furthest thing from Lori's mind was that this informal prescreening in a large roomful of friendly and wonderful four-year-olds on a sun-filled day might mark our son from the start of his education as unfit to be taught with "normal" children.

Was it usual to lie to us about the prescreening? Yes. Invariably, lies are part of the methodology of educational diagnosis and Special Education. We have since received and researched thousands of letters and accounts from educators, school psychologists, principals, district superintendents, and Special Education teachers—not to mention hospital and clinical child-development testers—that document lies to parents about tests on their children, about the legal ramification of signing "this little form," about the nature of the special training to be given to their children.

At one point in the prescreening of the innocents, Alec was given a test by a woman—a helper and not a psychologist—that consisted of forming a bridge with three blocks: two bottom blocks spanned by a third block. She demonstrated this crude bridge and asked Alec to repeat the test of his skill.

Alec smiled at her. He has a charming smile and something of a quiet smart-aleck manner like his mother's. As it turned out, Alec did a dumb thing on that innocent day. He took the first block, laid it down, took the second block and balanced it off-center with the first, and then balanced the third block off-center, on top of the second. It formed a bridge on its side or the letter *c*.

The woman tester told Lori that her son was "wrong." She marked down the "wrong" response on a piece of paper and called the school psychologist over. What was this about?

We would find out later that all the testers in the room were from the Special Education district that covered our town and nearby suburbs. We hadn't been told this. And the innocent prescreening program was to sort out children to be branded as "beyond" normal—and ready for Special Education.

Lori will never forget the response of the psychologist who came over, saw Alec's "wrong" response, and said to a fellow worker across the room: "I've got one, I've got one!"

Turning to Lori, he said that there was an indication that Alec "might not be normal" and that he would like to give him other tests. There was just a little form to sign. It was a formality. Wisely, Lori did not sign the form.

The street smarts of the girl raised in the inner city made her instinctively cautious all of a sudden. If a test was routine or a thing was intended to be "good" for a child, why did you have to agree to sign away certain parental rights to have it?

Too many don't hesitate, which is how thousands of kids get locked in the whole nightmarish pantheon of federally-funded and state-administered Special Education programs that have become a cruel joke on an entire generation of kids.

Special Ed—everyone uses the nickname—started out with the good intention of providing an education to the very small percentage of children with severe handicaps who might be left uneducated because their parents did not have enough money for private tutors or schools. This was the intent of the federal law passed in 1975.

Special Ed leaped in size overnight with the passage of Public Law 94-142 by Congress that year. The law is called the Education for All Handicapped Children Act. The law tried to guarantee a free education for children previously excluded from public schools: children with severe physical handicaps, children slightly or profoundly retarded, children with discipline problems.

Like all laws, it had flaws. At a time of decline in school enrollment and stubborn resistance to increased public education funding, Special Ed was suddenly a growth industry. Essentially, the law could give money to school districts to help "special" children. And the more special children found, the more money.

Parents are usually talked into placing their child in Special Education to cure a specific problem—Johnny can't read as fast as others, Johnny has trouble with his handwriting—and the parents are usually assured that their child will soon be back in a mainstream classroom. In fact, most such children stay in Special Ed for their school lives, learning how to live with their labels, learning to be failures.

Eleven years after passage of PL 94-142, nearly 80 percent of children in Special Ed are there not because of identified physical problems, but because of someone's feeling—a teacher's, a school social worker's, a psychologist's—that the child didn't act like other kids. Eighty percent.

Kids are put in programs for the emotionally disturbed, the retarded, the behavior-disordered or speech-disabled, or other amorphous categories on the basis of often vague, pseudoscientific, even fraudulent, criteria. To put it in plain English—and we have testimony from schoolteachers, principals, and administrators who agree totally—a lot of kids are placed in Special Ed programs because teachers thought the kids were "different."

The burden is on teachers, according to most experts. Experts say the main cause of misplacement of normal children in Special Ed programs is bad referrals from teachers who just don't want to bother teaching some kinds of children.

Often children with minor problems find themselves placed in dummy rooms or dummy schools with little hope of getting out. They find themselves sentenced to year-round schools (increasing for Special Ed kids) and spending hours each day on school buses taking them to far-flung "special" settings, where they are warehoused until they are eighteen.

Some examples from life are:

A child with a stuttering problem—not that uncommon—can be sentenced to Special Ed classes where he is in the company of children with severe discipline and behavioral problems. It is akin to a young man sentenced to jail for a first small crime being placed in the company of rapists and murderers.

A child who falls behind in math or reading in a given year can suddenly be whisked to the "special school" or quarantined in a normal school in what kids call with brutal directness "the dummy room."

The horror of Special Ed is that it is widespread and that its cruelties are so random.

For example, we would discover later that the township of Cook County, Illinois, where we lived had a Special Ed program at the time of Alec's testing that included *one* out of every *five* kids in public school. Nearly 20 percent of the kids were in Special Education, when the national average at the time was 10.1 percent (and that has since grown). However, if we had lived three miles south, we would have been in a different township where Special Ed labeling is not so relentless.

Dr. Howard Blackman, director of Special Education in that township, later told Lori the horror stories of Special Education are all too true: "Unfortunately, there have been incentives to label more and more children [as Special Ed kids]. The funding structure works on labels. But the labels aren't doing anything to educate kids, and they're hurting kids. I'm saying there are ways to get away from this label game."

Our nightmare was to fight to keep Alec from being labeled, to find out what specific learning problem he might have, and to find people in education who were not there to label kids or to "go along with the system," who were not trying to lie to us or to practice their specialties while wearing blinders. We did find some, finally, so this story is not a tragedy. And even nightmares end.

Bill was not concerned about the prescreening day or the psychologist's cry that he "got one." Bill is a product of Catholic schools and thought the problems of Special Ed could be avoided by enrolling Alec at the local Catholic school for kindergarten.

The psychologist at the prescreening had warned Lori that if Alec enrolled in kindergarten at the public school, the law said the Special Education district could mandate an evaluation of him. This means they could test him whether we wanted him tested or not. And the psychologist assured Lori that any such test would mean Alec would be placed in the Special Education program. So why should Lori fight the idea of signing a simple form?

Lori was uncertain for weeks. She was not a Catholic. She believed in the idea of public education. But the psychologist had shaken her. She wanted to do the right thing for Alec. She decided to examine the local Special Education school.

The school was located in nearby Westchester; we lived in Hillside. The school was a long bus ride from our home. The school had its own fleet of Special Ed buses, and all the special kids got on the Special Ed buses, while the "normal" kids of the neighborhood got to ride on the "normal" bus to the regular school.

Is kindergarten so important that children had to be prescreened for it? A lot of states think so. In Minnesota, under a controversial program begun two years ago, the public schools test children in kindergarten for their ability to do first-grade work—and those who fail the test are held back in kindergarten another year. And 10 percent actually fail kindergarten!

Supporters of such stressful tests argue that holding children back for an extra year of kindergarten guards the children against future failure. In other words—removing the educationese—you prevent future failures by failing kids early.

Actually, research that has been done on such programs so far does not support the prevention-of-failure argument: Kids allowed to move ahead with their age mates are less likely to end up in Special Ed in later years, according to several studies.

Lori finally became convinced of the horror of Special Ed in our district when she went to visit the facility in Westchester. She came home pale and shaken and depressed. She sat down across from Bill at the kitchen table and he poured her a cup of tea. She warmed herself and the color came back to her face.

She had been there for two hours. She said she had witnessed a large, cold, dirty classroom where all the books and toys were kept on high shelves out of the reach of children.

It had been a horrible spectacle. The room was filled with children. There were excited kids who could not sit still and ran around the room; aggressive kids bullying other kids; and kids pushing and shoving each other in the classroom under the unconcerned gaze of the Special Ed teachers. She saw some kids just sitting there, staring ahead of them, their faces showing that they were learning the lesson of hopelessness and failure.

She saw all this because she stood and chatted with three workers charged with supervising and teaching the special kids. There was nothing special at all, except the obvious neglect of the children and the odor of failure in the room.

The three women seemed charged with keeping the chaos in front of them in bounds. When they talked to the children, it was in loud voices and with bright and condescending smiles.

One woman pointed to a quiet boy sitting alone and said in a loud voice: "He's definitely brain-damaged." In the years to come, we found that offhand diagnoses—cruel as any adult utterance in a page of Dickens—were common in the profession of education.

Teachers could spot brain damage by the way a child sat. Teachers said that neurological damage was obvious in the way a child spoke. Teachers said severe retardation was obvious in the way a child drew a picture or colored outside the lines.

We later found that all Lori witnessed that day was the tip of an iceberg of indifference in Special Education. Some children are drugged routinely to make them quiescent. Some children are fed "treats" at intervals for good behavior, as if the children were being trained like dogs. Some children are given "aversion therapy"—they are locked in closets, struck, screamed at—to teach them not to do something the teacher thinks they shouldn't do.

Some children, sentenced to "dummy" schools for slight speech problems, come out of Special Ed almost like hardened criminals, having learned to deal harshly in a world they have had to survive.

Lori was convinced. Alec would be saved from the cruel world of Special Education. We would escape through the route of private education.

We had a lot to learn.

2

The Beginning
of the Fight

We try now to see Alec as he was. We look at the children
of other puzzled parents who are fighting labeling by Special Education dumping grounds, and we try to see the
good and bad in the children. We listen to often tearful
accounts from distraught parents who want the best education for their child but are confused by mumbo jumbo and
offhand psychological evaluations from paraprofessionals
who, quite simply, don't know what they're talking about.

Who was Alec at age four? He was a strong and healthy
boy, he was quite loving in little ways, he never threw a
tantrum and rarely resorted to tears of frustration. He had
problems not of his making. For instance, he was left-
handed in small-motor things such as eating and buttoning
his shirt, but he was right-handed in large-motor things
such as catching a ball.

He was slow to speak. His speech pattern worried us,

but not some of our older friends. Some of the old-timers in our families would advise: "Don't bother about it. He'll talk enough when he's got something to say."

Old-timers tend to go easy on things that make young children seem different. The modern trend is to accelerate education and evaluation so that three- and four-year-olds are already in positions where they have to prove they are normal and ready for normal education.

Alec's speech patterns continued to lag behind other kids his age, even in the normal school and good class environment that came at the end of his experience. Only by mere chance did we finally discover why and find out that it was easy to correct the problem. It is part of the frustration inherent in the nightmare of Special Ed that everyone has a diagnosis and a label ready to be attached, but so few of these labels and diagnoses have any relevance to the problem.

Alec spoke clearly enough but abruptly. He had trouble putting his large vocabulary in full sentences. He loved to play word games; they came naturally to him. Birthdays and birthday cakes became an Alec holiday in which he wished one and all "Happy Birthcake!" I am afraid we were delighted by his differences.

Bill had been slow to speak as a child. He had taken refuge in childhood's traditional shelters for loneliness— reading and daydreaming.

At about the age of four, Alec's eyes appeared to cross when he was tired. This peculiar phenomenon was eventually correctly diagnosed by a developmental optometrist and corrected, and as things turned out later, this was at the root of all of Alec's problems.

He liked other kids, and he got on well with them. He was an only child and he had a touching appreciation for the company of other kids. There he was, rangy, with broad shoulders and a shy smile—a Jimmy Stewart in miniature —with a zest for life and a sweet nature that melted most hearts that touched his.

We want to describe honestly what he was like to help

you understand all the horrors of misdiagnosis that would haunt his early years of education.

When he was five, we enrolled him in the local Catholic school. It was called St. Domitilla School, named for a mythical Roman matron who was the patron saint of cemeteries. The village we lived in was surrounded by cemeteries.

The school was two blocks from our house, even closer than the Hillside public school. The kindergarten class was enormous. The school seemed to be bursting at the seams. We later discovered that the free public school—with a wealth of special equipment and small classes—had a limp attendance, less than 20 percent the size of the local Catholic school. It is true that Chicago and the suburbs have an overwhelmingly large Catholic population, but other suburbs did not necessarily have such small public schools. They varied with the quality of the schools.

The kindergarten classroom was bright and cheerful despite the shopworn equipment. One elderly nun ran the class and was aided by a low-paid assistant named Mrs. S., who had never gone beyond high school but had learned a winning way with kids because she had raised three of them.

In the Montessori preschool, Alec had been introduced to a world of learning that was full of self-initiative and quiet self-discipline. The essence of the Montessori method is to teach children self-respect by respecting them in a nonthreatening, nonregimented way. As any Catholic school alum can assure you, the method is different in the Catholic system.

Alec was shocked by the rigid kindergarten system. There were extended periods of prayers and hymn singing that occupied the longest part of the morning. Because of the enormous number of children, they were arrayed in rows and told to sit up straight, hands on desks, and be quiet at all times, as they listened to old LP recordings of Bible stories.

The nun was of the old school and she moved constantly back and forth, keeping the lid on the squirming mass of five- and six-year-olds under her care. Three weeks into the school year, she conferred with us about our son. He had shouted out his frustrations, she said, and crawled under his desk.

Lori said, "He doesn't do that at home because we don't tolerate it. Tell him not to do it."

The nun seemed dumbfounded by the advice, but gave it a try. Wonder of wonders—it worked. In our long experience over the next few years, we found a remarkable reluctance on the part of most teachers to act as most parents would act when confronted by bad classroom behavior: Tell the child to stop acting up.

After his rocky beginning, Alec started learning the rules and learning his lessons. We have to say the Catholic school developed an affectionate hands-on approach to Alec and to other boys who were being boys more often than not.

Alec showed a quick grasp of reading but he clearly hated the reading materials. The materials were pathetic, as they frequently are in public and private schools. Nonsensical books about Mat the Rat were favored at St. Domitilla. Dr. Bruno Bettelheim, the retired University of Chicago professor of psychiatry, has called such material empty and condescending. Alec and the other kids who quickly picked up on reading were terribly bored by the texts.

(Our intimate acquaintance of life in the kindergarten came from Lori's observation. Throughout the year, she volunteered to help in the class once a week.)

Alec became class milkman. He was in charge of bringing in the school milk for the morning break. This kept him out of the class for a while, gave him the kind of individual responsibility he liked, and kept him away from a gang of other little boys who would rather goof off with each other than listen to songs about Jesus.

Alec responded most to the discipline and warmth of the assistant, Mrs. S. She had a straightforward and warm-hearted approach to the kids that they all found immediate and winning. At the end of the school year, Alec told us once: "I love Mrs. S. You know that?"

"We know."

"I like Sister U., too," the politician said.

"We know."

And in case we had missed the message, he added: "But I love Mrs. S." He wasn't the only one.

Halfway through the kindergarten year, one nun solemnly told my wife that it was clear to her that our son had "neurological problems" and the sooner we faced up to it, the better. She had based her judgment on a relative once diagnosed as having neurological problems, who sometimes acted like Alec. How did Alec act? He didn't pay attention at times. At times he talked to other kids in class when he was supposed to be silent.

Trendy terms—frequently misused—like *dyslexia, minimal brain damage, specific learning disabilities,* and *neurological dysfunction* are often on the lips of teachers who have very little idea of what they mean but know they want to decrease their class sizes by shipping off their problem kids to Special Education segregation. The judgments on the kids—who have little way to fight back—can be more cruel than vicious gossip.

Minimal brain damage or minimal brain dysfunction, for example, is in wide currency in the classrooms of the United States. Know what it means? It means that we can't find anything to explain a quirk of a kid's behavior, so there must be something wrong with his brain that we do not have the technology to discover. In short, it is utterly meaningless, but it can be used by educators to lock a kid in a program with other "brain-damaged" youngsters to make certain he is taught how to roller-skate and make Jell-O, instead of how to read and write.

Special Education teaches kids how to be failures and to live with being failures. It segregates kids from "normal" kids by putting special labels on them, putting them in separate classrooms, putting them in separate schools, and making certain that not too much is ever asked of them or expected of them.

After kindergarten, we decided not to continue at St. Domitilla. The nuns liked Alec, but not well enough to want to keep him in their school.

We enrolled Alec in Alexine Academy in a suburb seven miles from our home. The school has since closed down because of declining enrollment.

Alexine was on a rambling campus. It smelled like an old-fashioned school. The classrooms were full of dark woods and black blackboards, and there were piano-practice rooms and long corridors. The principal of the school wore the old-fashioned habit of her order of nuns.

It was summer when we talked to her. We wanted her to meet Alec. We talked about his small motor–coordination problems. His handwriting—printing—was atrocious. He had vision problems and we had gone to an ophthalmologist to have them corrected, but everything would take time. He was a left-hander and that didn't help his printing, as any left-hander can assure you. We told her Alec's pediatrician had said not to worry about his left-handed awkwardness and small-motor problems; she was of the "he'll outgrow it" school of child-rearing.

Our honest conversation with the principal ended with her taking Alec out alone for a walk on the school grounds. She talked directly to him in a gentle voice and we saw it was going to be all right.

After her time alone with Alec she said, "Alec seems to me to be a perfectly normal little boy, and we're going to get along fine at school. We always figure some first-graders need time to settle down."

We thought the nightmare was over.

In September, he started at Alexine. In the first week of school he brought home papers showing his strong start. The school program was a little behind his achievements in kindergarten, but he was eager to raise his hand in class and answer questions, according to the first-grade teacher.

A week or two later it changed. We were called to school. Alec had crawled under his desk when the teacher bore in on him. We told her that Alec had no discipline problems at home and that he would not have any at school. We came down on him like a ton of bricks. We told him the rules for the new school. And the first-grade teacher never reported a class disruption again. Kids want to know what the rules are.

Every day, after school, Lori or Bill would say: "Did you behave today?"

And Alec would look with open blue eyes and say: "No ton of bricks today."

As noted, his speech still lagged. Sometimes it seemed to us his thoughts were faster than his speech, as in the example of asking if he behaved. He was skipping the answer to go to the conclusion of the conversation, meaning there was no need for us to come down on him like a ton of bricks.

Lori became frenzied because of the continued hostility of the first-grade nun. The nun had no discipline problems with Alec. She just didn't want to deal with a "different" child. The sweet reasonableness of the principal of the school, who said Alec was going to get along fine, was replaced by the irrational hatred of a middle-aged woman who happened to be a nun.

A teacher who decides she doesn't like a kid in her class is in an almost invulnerable position of power. She can make it harder on a kid than the most tyrannical boss in the most backward business can come down on an employee. Employee rights have multiplied in the last twenty years. Kids in classrooms are little changed from Dickens's days, save for rules against physical abuse.

About this time, Lori began to read everything she could on the subject of learning and on kids who had learning problems. And that is when we first began to find out that there is a growing debate over the way we teach kids, label kids, and test kids, and that the range of what is called normal grows narrower and narrower.

One of the first books she ran across was Stephen Jay Gould's *The Mismeasure of Man*. It destroyed the pseudo-scientific basis for our commonly accepted IQ (intelligence quotient) tests. We wouldn't know then that it was our turn to be subjected to the mumbo jumbo of the intelligence labelers.

We were called to Alexine in October for a conference with the first-grade nun. We wanted to know what was wrong. The first-grade nun was tight-lipped and her face was angry and red.

"I think you know what's wrong," she said, and she literally threw a coloring paper at Lori. It was one that Alec had done. As usual, Alec had colored out of the lines. We had explained this to the principal and the first-grade nun at the beginning of the school year. Give him time, we said.

Besides, Bill thought that coloring out of the lines was not the gravest error one might make in the educational process. He was having a problem taking the hostility of the nun with seriousness.

"Any child who colors like that at six and a half is retarded," the first-grade nun said to us.

Lori's face went white. She was shocked. She spoke calmly but her words were flat. Give him time, she said. Just give him a little time.

The nun seemed to calm down. She was a strange person in many ways, with violent swings of temperament. She suddenly asked if it would be all right if one of the young lay teachers recently out of school gave Alec special speech help along with other kids with speech problems.

We agreed. Alec had gone with other kids in the kindergarten at St. Domitilla to a speech class in the school.

The nun said that before the speech classes, we would have to agree to some tests to see how to help Alec's speech difficulties. We would have to sign some papers. And, she added, we had to agree that Alec was not mature enough to sign up for piano lessons, as Lori had wanted.

Yes, yes, yes, we agreed. And we signed. In retrospect, it is obvious the nun lied to us from the first.

A week later, we went back to Alexine for a conference. The conference included the principal, who had found Alec such a normal little boy in the summer. It included the first-grade teacher, who had a sheaf of papers to present in evidence. The papers consisted of Alec's drawings and colorings. The young paraprofessional tester was also present. She told us that she had a course in learning how to administer tests in college and that she had given Alec a number of tests that proved to her that he was retarded.

She said her tests proved that Alec's mental age was three. That he had an IQ, therefore, that hovered around 50. That Alec was an imbecile.

We sputtered protest.

The young woman continued calmly. Her tests, she said, proved that Alec did not know shapes and colors. That he did not know the letters of the alphabet. That he did not know how to count.

We were stunned. He had done all that easily in preschool—one of the first. And he could read, we pointed out.

It didn't matter. The tests were what mattered. There was nothing in the tests to show that he knew his alphabet.

But he can read!

Well, that was true, the trio admitted. But that was not important; the test results were what counted. The tests had not been designed to find out how to help Alec's slow speech problem. They had been administered as a way to get him out of Alexine Academy. And the test results were obviously invalid but that did not matter, not to any of them.

Bill said he looked at the principal in that moment and saw such a look of cynical intelligence that he hated her. She knew what was going on. The child would be sacrificed to appease the erratic first-grade nun, so that the school could be run without making waves. The cards had been marked and stacked before the conference began.

In Christian charity, the nun said, Alec would be permitted to remain in first grade at the school until we arranged to transfer him to some special school where he could be helped. He would not be taught, we were told—that would be useless. But since Alec presented no discipline problems, he could remain in school for a while, sit with the kids, listen to lessons, and play with them at recess. (Obviously, this ended up making Alec a class celebrity and envy of other little boys burdened with tests and homework.)

In the evening, Lori began to teach Alec at home, sitting at the kitchen table. She had taught at the university level and now she was teaching at the more important level —at first-grade level. There were books to read and numbers to add, and he bore it all with patience and love. He brought home no papers because he was asked to do nothing. Nothing was expected of him anymore by anyone at Alexine, except that he go away in time.

We were told to have Alec tested by professionals at a hospital. There are many professional centers where children are tested and we went to one of the best—Northwestern University Evaluation Center for Learning at Evanston Hospital in Evanston, Illinois. The procedure was supposed to be among the most thorough in the country. We wanted to see if there was something wrong with Alec and, if so, what it was and how we could help him. We thought his problems had to do with his eyes and his left-handedness, and we wanted to make it all right for him.

We did not want to be arrogant and conclude he was all right if he was in trouble. But every time we had turned to a teacher for help, we had received nonsensical diagnoses: He didn't know his alphabet (but he could read), he could not recognize numbers (but he could add and subtract), he colored outside the lines (something that was sure to stop him from rising in the corporate world as an adult).

And then came the blackest part of the nightmare that never seemed to end.

3

Testing Alec

The reason we went to the hospital in Evanston was that because we were going to pay for the testing, we thought they would be more honest than the local school district would be. We still remembered the happy psychologist who had cried "I've got one! I've got one!"

We had discovered that the local Special Education district could gain more than $4,000 a year in salaries and contracts and supplies, if it succeeded in putting Alec in full-time Special Education. Because Special Education has so much federal and state support, it has become a very lucrative program.

We were living about thirty urban miles from Evanston. We went there several times over that long and terrible autumn. The psychologists in the testing center seemed in no great hurry. Actually, they were very busy and that is why the sessions were scheduled over a long period of time. There are many, many children who are tested for learning disabilities and signs of retardation at places like this.

While the autumn passed, Lori read all that she could on the problems of Special Education. She even read *Teach Your Own* by the late John Holt, a teacher who had broken with the education system and who came to believe that there is so much fraud in our educational system that a child would be better off out of the system. John Holt called learning disabilities "an imaginary disease."

Lori wrote to the Calvert School in Maryland, which provides teach-by-mail courses for Americans who live abroad. If we could not find a school for Alec where he would be allowed to learn and grow—and it seemed that way at the time even though we lived in the second-largest metropolitan area in the country—we would keep him home and teach him ourselves.

We knew that some people who had taken their children out of school had been threatened with truancy proceedings and we were willing to chance that. We even thought about leaving the country.

Lori had spoken to the people at Northwestern before we took Alec there. She had been attracted to a statement by one of their staff who said the center was willing to fight a school district to keep a child out of Special Education, if that is what the tests at the center indicated.

(We would find out much later that all of the evaluators at the center previously had worked for public school districts on child-study committees of the sort that researchers have found are "rubber stamp" committees, affirming a teacher's opinion of a child's learning abilities.)

The procedure at the center was warm and homely. We were put in a conference room where the walls were covered with drawings by children.

Lori and I tried to be honest with the staff. We balanced our concern about Alec's laconic speech habits with his good points. He was not hyperactive and not a stick-in-the-mud. He never threw a tantrum. He ate well, played jokes on us, and told jokes involving childish puns. He loved the way similar sounds came from different words. (He still does and loves poetry.) He loved to shorten words into other words, creating new words like *Birthcake.* It is not that he did not understand *birthday* and *cake,* but that he delighted in the new sound of the new word.

We gave them an example. His step-grandfather liked to tickle him under the arms. He calls this man Chuck. One night, describing being tickled by Chuck, Alec said: "This guy gets me under the arms and he chuckles me."

We told them everything. Alec had been the first kid in his preschool to know his numbers and letters. He rode his bike all over the neighborhood and always came home on time. He was a good reader and he loved books in a house that was full of books to be loved.

They gave Alec a physical. They gave him a CAT scan. The battery of psychologists gave him test after test.

Fall became a Chicago winter, dark and full of small days. We tried to talk to friends and neighbors and family about the problems we were having. We saw them shrink away from us. Our problem was in not accepting something they thought the "experts" knew more about. You could see it in their eyes. Alec must be peculiar if someone thought he was peculiar. You could see they loved Alec, that he got along with everyone in the family situation, but there came a time when you had to listen to the experts.

Finally, two months after the tests began, we were called into the conference room at the hospital again. Alec was left out in the hall.

The pediatric specialist said there was nothing physically wrong with Alec, save for an obvious eye problem, but since he wore glasses, it was assumed it was being corrected.

And then the shrinks had their turn. They had a piece of paper that summarized their findings. We still have it. I think I will give it to Alec as a graduation present when he gets out of college. The tests concluded beyond question that Alec had an IQ of 47.

It was roughly what the young tester at Alexine Academy had concluded. (The testers had promised not to contact the school or consult with them in reaching their independent diagnosis but, oddly, when we got a bill from the hospital, it itemized charges for consulting with the school. Either the bill was a lie or the testers were liars.)

They let the number 47 sink in for a moment, and then one of them said the figure was probably high because it was obvious that Alec had "pushed" to reach that level. She said that it would probably turn out that his "cognitive developmental age" was between two and three; he was nearly seven at the time.

In the old terminology of the IQ test, when the language was more brutal, Alec tested out to be an imbecile. In the new, softer terminology, Alec was eight points down in the category called "trainable mentally handicapped." TMH. To understand this term, listen to the Encyclopaedia Britannica article on learning problems. It says children in the TMH range "do not profit from scholastic instruction."

In other words, they are so severely retarded that their future should be one of sheltered care and development of self-help skills, such as learning to tie their shoelaces and learning to keep their bodies clean.

One widely used textbook for educators who work with TMH children advises that parents should be counseled out of insisting their children be taught to read more than Stop signs or Exit signs, since true reading is simply impossible at this IQ level.

The chief psychologist—a Ph.D. this time—said our happy and sociable little boy was severely emotionally disturbed and "holding on to the thin edge of reality." A second in the room said a school such as the Joseph Kennedy School in the Chicago suburbs for the severely retarded would be a "safe" place to put Alec, because he would never be asked to do things there "we know he cannot do."

The trap of Special Education was now open and waiting for the little boy. It is a beguiling trap. Children of Special Education are children of Small Expectations, not great ones. Little is expected and little is demanded. Gradually, these children—no matter their IQ level—learn to be cozy in the category of being "special." They learn to be less than they are.

We cannot ever forget the horror of that dark morning in that bright and cheerful conference room, where the walls are decorated with the drawings of children.

TMH was one category below EMH, which stands for "educable mentally handicapped" in the new terminology (and moron in the old terminology). Experts say that perhaps 1 percent of the school population might be in the EMH category. We would discover that in Illinois alone some districts have more than four times that proportion labeled EMH. How is it possible? Some districts label 8 to 9 percent of their black kids as EMH. And teachers in a recent national survey said 23 percent of their students should be in programs for the handicapped!

Alec was being given a sentence of living death that morning. We heard the sentence. We were to return the following week, after we had "grieved," and we would be told the schools to which we might apply.

We left with our little boy, who had waited for us in the hospital corridor. We went downstairs and out into winter and got into the truck and started for home. Alec sat next to his mother and he stared at her with his deep and now somber blue eyes, and he saw the terror in his mother's pale face. He touched her nose with the palm of his hand and said, "Beep, beep."

His mother smiled at him and her eyes were wet.

"It's all right, Mamma," he said. He was smiling at her to cheer her up.

"I love you,' she said. Her heart was broken.

"Everything's all right," Bill lied. It is his way. Alec reached across the front seat and gave the driver a "Beep, beep" as well.

Our tears came after Alec slept. Bill poured himself Scotch and waited for the stupor, because the shock was wearing off and the pain was beginning. He remembered when he had cut his kneecap as a kid and there had been no pain for a long time, though the cut was open and muscle and bone was visible. There had been no pain until night, and then the pain had gone on and on and on.

We kept all the lights on in the house that night to keep away the bogeyman that waits in the darkness. We talked and talked and wondered how it could be that Alec was so retarded.

God gave us the next morning to see things anew. We felt stronger. We talked about Alec and we talked about his reading. Bill wondered whether they had actually had the boy read. Lori said they must have—we had insisted over and over that he was a good reader, a bright child with an interest in books. She remembered the phone call she had made a couple of weeks before, during that long time when these people would not talk to us, would not put an end to their testing. She had talked to the head of the center, asking how the testing was going. Was the boy demonstrating his reading, responding properly to them? Would they like her to come in and show how well he worked with her?

"Oh, no," the director had assured her. "We are getting very good responses. He's working very well with our people. We are certain we're going to have some good answers for you."

There had been something wrong, then, we both thought. Something wrong with people who were getting "good responses" one week and a few weeks later were finding a child too retarded to respond to age-level tasks at all. The more we talked the more we thought something very strange was going on.

So, on Saturday, we realized we would have to bring

proof to the evaluation center to show that Alec could read. It was not only the reading, of course; the child could do other things very well, too, as we had explained. But we were beginning to see that no one believed us. The reading would be easily proved.

We were to find out later that parents are frequently not believed by psychotesters—all those people, public and private, who think children can be pinned down and labeled by giving them tests or having "experts" judge their personalities or interpret some tiny sample of their behavior. Parents are not believed because they are not "objective" about their children.

Glenn Doman, who has worked with children with demonstrable brain injuries for years, has encountered this problem. "The unspoken law holds that all mothers are idiots and they have no truth in them. The tragic consequences of this is that almost no professional people talk to mothers, and God knows that almost nobody listens to them. What makes this so especially sad is that mothers know more about their own children than anyone else in the world."

Doman says that after years of working with parents on often strenuous rehabilitation programs, he has become convinced parents are not the problem with children, but the solution. But this is a decidedly heretical opinion in the world of education and child evaluation.

That Saturday morning, Bill produced a small Panasonic tape recorder and turned it on in the kitchen of the house where we then lived. Alec was reading. In the tape, you can hear Lori at the sink doing dishes. It was painful to Bill and he was afraid he would distract Alec by hovering over him, so he left the house. But he still has the tape.

In the tape, Alec reads a story from an English reader we had picked up in Paris. In the reader, which is geared to roughly the third-grade level (and Alec was in first grade), a boy and a girl visit a farm. You can hear Alec's slightly nasal voice pick through the story. On the tape, you can hear Lori asking him from time to time what he has just read. And you can hear Alec answer in other words.

Two days later, we went to the conference room again. Bill started to speak of Alec's ability to read, but the motherly chief psychologist interrupted with a look of pity.

"Mr. Granger. You are too ego-involved with the child to be objective. Alec has no prereading skills. Our tests showed that."

"But we told you the first day that he could read."

The woman smiled in condescension at the parents who would not accept the grieving process.

"Which of you asked him to read?" Lori asked.

The psychotesters looked at each other, still smiling. No one had, they explained gently. Knowing he could not, it would have been "cruel" to ask him to read.

Why had Alec failed the tests?

We don't know. We know now that he had more severe eye problems than we guessed (and more easily corrected once we had the right diagnosis). We know that kids can approach tests badly. We had seen that the puzzling smiles of the testers had frightened the boy every bit as much as they disturbed us. We know that an ability to pass tests proves nothing more than the ability to pass tests. We think Alec was terrorized by the procedures, by strangers probing him with questions, by endless questions. Was it terror from a hostile nun that had made him crawl under his desk those first weeks in first grade? Who can probe the true terrors of children in the hands of hostile strangers?

The staff would admit later that instead of seeing if Alec could read as we said, they had given him IQ tests to pinpoint retardation. If he wasn't retarded, we would not have asked for the tests in the first place. There is no such thing as a "checkup" in this branch of medicine.

We played the tape and gave the English reader to the chief psychologist. She followed along as Alec's voice came off the tape, reading strongly. Her smile of pity became frozen. She was listening to a boy with an IQ of 47—an imbecile "holding on to the thin edge of reality"—reading above his age level.

When it was over, one of the secondary shrinks said that it didn't prove that he wasn't retarded. Bill stared at him as though he had just revealed he was a Martian.

The chief psychologist broke in at that point. Perhaps she even understood the absurdity of their diagnosis. She said there was obviously some problem here and that the child would have to be evaluated again to find out what was really wrong with him. She spoke in the manner of a surgeon who has just operated on a person for bad tonsils and removed his spleen instead and then suggests a second operation to correct the error.

That cracked it for us. From that moment we would have no more recourse to spirits and shrinks and other promoters of self-fulfilling prophecies. From articles written about our experience, we would receive an overwhelming body of letters supporting us and citing similar experiences, but we would still get oddball letters like the one from a California psychologist who said that she read a four-page condensed account written by Bill in *Reader's Digest* and could conclude from a distance of 2,300 miles that Alec might not seem retarded now but would be later in life.

We knew everyone had been wrong, part of a cozy conspiracy of lies. We continue to be haunted to this day, wondering about the thousands and thousands of misdiagnosed kids who are rotting away in Special Education schools or homes for the retarded, who were misdiagnosed as casually as Alec was misdiagnosed.

(We were given a bill for $897 and refused to pay Evanston Hospital. They said they would sue. We said we welcomed the suit. We never heard from them again. We have kept all the correspondence with the hospital, including the extraordinary letter from the chief psychologist admitting the diagnosis was wrong and saying why they never asked Alec to read.)

This time we left the hospital without tears. We were just angry, both of us. We went out to Alexine Academy for the last time to pick up Alec's gym clothes. They had been taken from the locker and folded neatly and a rosary had been placed on top of the pile of clothes. Lori took the rosary and threw it to the floor.

Bill was shaken. He had been raised a Catholic, he had gone to Catholic schools all the way through college. If he had doubts as an adult, he had not joined that noisy and tiresome brigade of ex-Catholics who have to work up their anger daily against their old faith. But he was hurt by the rejection of Alec by the Church. Alec had been baptized a Catholic and the Church had taught that parents had to sacrifice to give their children a Catholic education. Bill's mother and father, considerably down in the economic classes, had struggled to send him and his siblings to Catholic schools, because it was the right thing to do.

The rules had changed, he thought then. The Church did not have to sacrifice or accept kids who might be Catholic but who also might be different.

When the story of Alec became public, literally thousands of people called and wrote to tell similar horror stories. Most touching were stories of Catholic parents who had been shut out of sending their kids to the Catholic school because this nun or that priest had decided Johnny or Alice was "weird" or "stuttered too much" or was "retarded." Suffer the little children—as long as they "color in the lines."

We did not turn our backs on the Catholic schools; they turned their backs on us. Bill still feels a deep bitterness about that.

4

Working the System

We went to the Hillside public school in December to enroll Alec. We were very tough now. We told the principal
exactly what had happened to Alec at Alexine Academy and
at Evanston Hospital and about the misdiagnosis. We said
we wanted no nonsense about Special Education. We said
we would fight it tooth and nail and make more trouble for
him than he would ever want.

He listened to us in a reasonable way. He called in one
of the two first-grade teachers. It was a wonderfully posh
school with extremely small classes, a tiny enrollment,
many facilities that would have made a high school proud,
and all sorts of special teachers for art and music and gym.
One would have thought more residents in the village
would have sent their kids to this free school instead of
struggling to push them into overcrowded classes at the
Catholic school. But they all warned us in the same voice:

Don't send a kid to the public school because he (or she) won't learn a thing.

We didn't expect him to be taught much. We wanted him to be left alone and we would take care of his education ourselves.

The principal of the public school, who listened to us so kindly, said at the end of the meeting that he would like the test results from Evanston Hospital.

We said the tests had just been proven wrong and that the testers who gave them agreed they were wrong.

He understood that, but he said wrong test results were better than nothing. He said they would be useful "for planning the child's future."

We would run into this incredible obtuseness among educators again and again. Bill once spoke to a meeting of Special Educators and pointed out the invalidity of the standard IQ test—that it was a meaningless test with a meaningless result. One of the Special Educators said in response, "It is invalid—we all know that—but it's just one of the tools we can use to help children." In another case, we ran across a celebrated Catholic school principal who said he studied handwriting among children to predict those who might later try to commit suicide. Quackery is alive and well in education.

The first-grade teacher seemed unhappy to welcome a new child into her class. She had all of seventeen children. She told us later that she had started the year with twenty-one, but had shipped off four to the local Special Education warehouse. She told Lori after eight school days that Alec should be sent there as well.

We were urged to sign a release required by law to permit new testing of Alec, so that he could be placed in Special Education. If we did not sign, the principal said, we could be overruled by an administrative hearing. We wearily refused to sign.

A month passed. Alec was getting tough also. We supported him and he understood that. He held his own in class. He didn't make waves and he didn't cause problems. He was learning the lesson of go along, get along.

An evaluation meeting was called. We objected. They said they would hold it without us. The principal made it clear that he would be glad to make decisions about our son's future without us present—that it was only because of certain annoying provisions in the law that we had been notified.

We arrived for the morning meeting armed with a tape recorder. This startled the principal badly. The meeting was designed to be stacked against us, not to be recorded.

Alec's teacher was there. So was the school social worker, the art teacher, the music teacher, the gym teacher —all with nothing better to do on a school day at ten in the morning.

We should point out that Alec had not been reported as having any behavior problems. Lori had gone out of her way to tell Ms. K., the first-grade teacher, to report any behavior problems. Lori had gone to the school every afternoon at three to pick Alec up and to ask Ms. K. if everything was all right. It had been all right all month.

Suddenly everything changed at the evaluation meeting. Ms. K. said Alec hit other kids all the time. He used "inappropriate speech" at times. He did not recite the "Pledge of Allegiance" (instead, he was saying the "Our Father," which he had mixed up with the Pledge at the local Catholic school).

This was the first we had heard of these problems. We asked how often Alec hit kids.

"Five or ten times a day," Ms. K. said.

There had been twenty school days in the month, Bill said, his voice rising. This meant he had hit other kids at least two hundred times in four weeks. Bill said Ms. K. was either the worst teacher in the world not to report this or she was a liar. Bill said he thought she was probably just a liar.

Ms. K. began to cry at that; it was good to make her cry. We wished, in that moment, we could have made them all cry.

The guerrilla war in public school continued for the rest of the year. The public school gave us an insight into what passes for public education in some districts.

Alec could read as well or better than anyone in the class. He had trouble seeing the blackboard. The blackboard was the heart of Ms. K.'s instruction methodology. The children, she said, were being taught "copying skills."

Each day, they were given a sentence on the board to copy and told to draw a picture to illustrate the sentence. This occupied a considerable part of what passed for schoolwork.

The sentences were sickening at times, often in praise of apple-polishers in the class. For example: "Mary is the best student of the month because she is always quiet in class."

Some were vaguely propagandistic, of the sort shallow teachers indulge in to make them feel socially responsible and politically aware: One warned that nuclear waste was dangerous to your health.

One of the classic copying exercises came after a field trip to Chicago's Museum of Science and Industry, where they keep the captured World War II German U-Boat, the *U-505*. The sentences read: "We went to the Museum of Science and Industry today. We went on a U.S. submarine."

On the other hand, we joked that Nazi symbols probably look familiar to someone who boasted that she shipped off a quarter of her first-grade class to the Special Education warehouse in less than three months, with nary a squeak of protest from parents.

We did not waste the year. We taught Alec at home. Alec played with his friends after school.

Lori found a private music teacher at Elmhurst College, who was also an accomplished concert performer. She told Louise Mangos about Alec's problems of eyesight and coordination. Louise Mangos, a striking dark-haired woman of exceptional vitality, said she wanted to give Alec a chance. Just a chance.

Alec took to the music quickly. His hands moved over the keys slowly at first, and then with more understanding. Louise Mangos said she was delighted; after a year, she rated Alec's sense of pitch and grasp of the intellectual fundamentals of music highly. His problems with following the notes on a page were, to her, intellectually intriguing. It became obvious as the boy struggled with the notes he so obviously understood when he heard them that his eyes were not working well for him—but the music was.

Louise Mangos was music to our ears and Alec waxed in self-confidence and pride because of her. At this writing, he is still her student, very much into boogie-woogie, jazz, and Bach.

We spent the rest of that year trying not to be bitter, trying to find a place for Alec to grow after public school let out. The principal continued to harass us with letters and telephone threats to get legal hearings to remove Alec from his school, because that is what the first-grade teacher wanted.

Alec helped us hold on to our sense of reality. He would do this great hug in which he grabbed Lori around the waist and grabbed Bill and pulled them together and buried his face in their bellies and, thus encircled, said: "We're Three Grangers. Always Three Grangers."

And Lori taught Alec in her own way. She taught him the stories of the Bible at night and taught him about Hercules and the Augean stables (which still greatly impresses him). He started to learn to speak French. He took swimming lessons and gymnastics lessons and did well. We were lucky to be on flexible schedules and to have time for Alec and time to fight the education bureaucracy.

A few years before, when Alec was four, he had discovered Winnie-the-Pooh and identified with Tigger, who is slightly disreputable and who is allowed to bounce because that is what Tiggers do best. "I'm Tigger," he said one day, and we let him be Tigger.

Slowly, the year passed.

5

Aftermath of a Nightmare

After a long and terrible search, we found a school, a principal, and a teacher who would give Alec a chance, just as Ms. Mangos had given him a chance. It was a small Montessori school close to the city. It was a wonderful, homemade school. It was full of black kids and Pakistani kids and Indian kids and Mexican kids and white kids. It was a tattered, poor, wonderful school with a broken gym floor and no PA system and an urgent need—according to the principal— in the office for a typewriter that worked. It was a struggling, down-at-the-heels, and smiling-at-the-mouth sort of school.

"I don't work miracles," the principal had said. His name was Larry Lewis and he was another Dickensian character, kindhearted, clear-eyed, faintly disorganized, and somewhat shy. But he had the guts to give a kid a chance:

"We give kids a chance." It was all Alec needed, not to have someone expect him to fail.

The Montessori method was devised by Maria Montessori, who taught Roman slum children after World War I. They were children considered hopeless, and Maria Montessori devised unusual ways to teach them so that they would not be hopeless—and a lot of her ways worked. Montessori emphasizes discipline that comes from common politeness among children and from treating each other with respect.

The first day he came home from school and his eyes were shining and we knew it would work. He said the magic words: "They treated me like a grown-up!"

It was all he had ever wanted.

It is three years later and Alec grows now in another Montessori school. He is a fine little boy and he has great expectations from himself and from his life to come.

There was difficulty after we had found the little Montessori school. Alec spent a long year learning that he was not about to be expelled or sent to a "dummy school." He learned a new set of rules in school based on the idea that the teacher did not intend to ambush him into making a mistake. It was difficult to learn trust again—for him and for us. What could not be relearned by any of us was a belief that somehow these special programs for special kids were intended for the best. Instead, as we continued our research into the arcane subject, we discovered that the Special Education system in this country was being used to build education empires, being used to manipulate racial patterns in suburban schools, being used for a number of purposes beyond the purpose intended by the public law of 1975.

In two years—between the ages of five and seven—our little boy was probed, tested, bullied, harassed, ignored, lied to—all by a vast assemblage of people who assured his parents they did it for his best interest. They were teachers, doctors, administrators. If this happened to us, what worse things happened to others? The question haunted us as we saw Alec grow in mind and confidence in the classrooms of the little Montessori school.

The rest of this book is not about Alec but about what happened to us when we decided to tell our story. The decision to speak out about Special Education and our nightmare came reluctantly, nearly a year after Alec left public school.

Bill wrote books and also a thrice-weekly column for the *Chicago Tribune*. Lori, who had done all the research on the subject, urged him to use the column to tell the story of Alec, so that other parents who might be in a similar nightmarish situation could see that sometimes the good guys win out by perseverance.

Bill was not eager to do so. We had won, so why tell everyone about it?

Lori urged him this way: "What's the use of having a column if you can't do good with it once in a while?"

Reluctance to air our story came from the strange sense of isolation that the three-year ordeal had given us. What good would it do Alec or any of us to tell this horror story to other people?

We thought about that for a long time and realized at last that if this thing had happened to us—middle-class, white, well-educated, and reasonably intelligent adults who were willing to fight on behalf of their child and with the luxury of time to continue the fight—what must it be like for others? If they were doing it to us, they were doing it to others. There was some moral obligation finally to tell the truth, even if it was painful to tell.

Bill eventually wrote a series of columns detailing what you have just read. He gave them to F. Richard Ciccone, the managing editor of the paper. Ciccone and James B. Squires, editor of the paper, conferred about the columns. They were tough, they named names, they were direct and unsettling, and they rocked the education establishment.

Ciccone and Squires agreed to run the columns. The columns ran on over three weeks. The reaction was startling.

First, there were letters: letters and letters that poured into the *Tribune* newsroom in a seemingly endless stream; thousands of letters, an unprecedented barrage of mail over one subject. The letters told similiar horror stories—and stories even more horrible. They told of kids trapped in Special Education classrooms for years because of wrong diagnoses; of kids denied private school education by religious groups and even some Montessori schools because the kids were considered "too weird." There were also letters from parents of children who wanted specific Special Education help—and were denied it by indifferent school districts. The letters came from teachers fed up with an inept school system, and they signed their names and gave their addresses. The letters came from principals and school administrators from all over the Midwest (the columns were carried only in the *Tribune* and were not syndicated). The letters have not stopped to this day; three years after those columns, two or three letters still arrive every week at the *Tribune,* talking about abuses of Special Education.

There were other reactions as well. For several mornings, on the front lawn of our house, there appeared spray-painted messages on cardboard that carried Nazi symbols; 666 (identified as "the number of the beast"); and crude depictions of stick figures representing Lori, Alec, and Bill and threatening death. The truck parked on the driveway was spray-painted. A local tavern-keeper told Bill that he deserved to be vandalized "for saying bad things about the Church in the newspaper." There were rocks thrown through the kitchen window. Eggs were thrown against the garage door. The garage door got a streak of spray paint.

We sold the house Alec had grown up in and moved out of the village. Not everyone in Hillside hated us—in fact, the police, the mayor, the woman in the delicatessan who had had similar experiences at the public school with her son—all supported us. But if there are only a few haters and everyone else is silent, then the haters can win.

We received letters stirred up in organized campaigns by teachers' and parents' groups to have Bill fired from his column. The *Chicago Tribune* printed the other side of the controversy, and it raged for months. Bill was not fired from his column.

We received hundreds of letters of support, particularly from some courageous teachers, principals, administrators, and school-system superintendents. We discovered groups concerned with the same Special Education problems we had been fighting alone.

And about a year after the column, we received a little note from a man named Dr. Daniel Nast, who had a small optometry shop on a shabby street in the suburb of Melrose Park. He said he had just read the columns and he thought he knew what was wrong with Alec. Another quack, we thought, but Lori went to see him.

He tested Alec in a gentle way and said that Alec could not see from left to right without changing from one eye to another. It was that simple. This was at the root of all his left-right problems, his speech problems, his small-motor problems. Dr. Nast said he could correct the problem with a few months of treatments. He said a lot of children had this problem, that the problem had been recognized for more than forty years, and that treatment was inexpensive and rather quick. It seemed incredible—we had been to ophthalmologists who had suggested dangerous eye operations, who had said there was nothing wrong with Alec's eyes . . . and here was a simple optometrist who said he could solve Alec's problems.

The treatment was rather playful and we thought we would give it a try. A therapist simply worked on a series of exercises three days a week (an hour per session) to get Alec to focus with both eyes at the same time. It was extraordinary! In three months, Alec's speech suddenly became clearer than it had been before, his attention span was greater, his reading leaped ahead, his handwriting improved.

How could it have been so simple a solution? And how could we have gotten so close to believing that our son was hopelessly retarded?

We have written this book to tell our painful story once again because someone has to stand up and be counted. As Jack Hinneberry, a suburban school principal, told us:

> I realize having worked with youngsters for thirty-two years that there are some who do need special help and in some rare instances, special placement. But I also realize that since Public Law 94-142 [the Special Education law], their number has increased dramatically. Every month, I give my speech of frustration as to why in God's name we are talking about classifying this child because he reverses his *b*'s or because he can't write on a line or because of this or that, when, in reality, another year or two on this earth will take care of the problem? And what are we going to do in thirty-minute LD sessions [learning-disability classes] four or five times a week that can't be done in the regular classroom?

In fact, that was what our son needed—a chance to grow up a little. Even optometrists in the specialty that helped Alec acknowledge that many kids with eye problems find a way to get around them as they grow up—if they have not been hopelessly demoralized by their experiences with schools by then.

Kids essentially need to be encouraged and need to be given a chance to enjoy the idea of growing up and learning new things. Special Education stands against that—as it currently is applied in the school system.

All kids need an education that is special, because all kids are different. They learn at different times and in different ways. Special Education should be an attempt to help a kid realize all he or she can be—not to label a kid with faulty information, using invalid tests, and to ware-

house him or her away so that more federal and state m‚
ies can be sopped up by a lazy, arrogant education bureau‚
racy that keeps producing generations of failures.

As Laura Rushakoff, a former Special Education teacher, put it to us: "Special Education has, today, become the dumping ground for any child who doesn't follow the norm—whatever that term may be. I have observed that Special Ed teachers, after a few years, take on a special quality that does not allow their vision to expand to accept eccentricity or creativity as a factor in human life."

An active Special Education teacher, Karen Schultz of Chicago, wrote that "I have tried many a time [as an LD teacher] to prevent a child from being placed with me. Too many regular-education teachers are too lazy and uncommitted to their jobs to teach anyone one step above or below the so-called norm."

We even got a letter from a black man named Ted Seals who had once been a newspaper colleague of Bill's. He revealed that he had been in Special Education in Chicago for two years.

"I ultimately graduated from Yale with a bachelor's degree in political science, so my advice to others is—don't let the ugly past get you down. Teachers know Special Education is a racket, but the more dedicated among them try to make it work for the children stuck in it. There are some dedicated Special Ed teachers out there." (Ted also wanted to add that he was placed in an "educable mentally handicapped" category for those in the under 70 IQ range —not bad for an eventual Yale University graduate.)

Special Education has become a rush to judgment and Special Education classes and schools have become dumping grounds for tomorrow's expected failures. Special Education teaches failure—as the psychologists at Northwestern University wrote us in the case of Alec, it would have been "cruel" to ask him to do more than they thought he could do. Wasn't it more cruel to set their expectation of him too low?

And what about kids with problems like cerebral palsy,

Down's syndrome, true autism (as opposed to the phony autistic syndromes bandied about by lazy Special Ed teachers to explain why kids don't pay attention in class)—what happens to them? Sadly, we got more response from parents of these kids, who told heartrending stories of administrators' indifference, inferior programs, physical punishments disguised as "aversion therapy," and rigid enforcement of low achievement on kids never given a chance because of some physical or mental handicap.

Some in Special Education argue that Special Ed classes are small and that a small-class environment can help kids, even if they have wildly different problems. This is nonsense. Even common sense says it is easier to help one or two slow readers adjust in a larger normal classroom setting than to throw into one dumping bin all the kids convicted of the crime of being different.

Special Education is out of control. Some districts have a third of all kids in Special Education and other districts have less than 5 percent—while the national Special Ed average hovers above 11 percent.

Is it possible that Special Ed numbers are being inflated by cash-poor school districts? The head of Special Education in Illinois recently admitted that this was the case—and then added it was understandable, because districts need money.[1]

Some school systems are rethinking Special Education today. Los Angeles is debating whether this rush to grade and sort and classify and label kids when they are very young is not a kind of total system failure.

Some people said to us: Look, what happened to you and your child was a tragedy and it is too bad, but it is not typical of the system of Special Education. If it is not typical of what is happening in Special Education today, then we must be the unluckiest people who have ever lived on earth, and those thousands of letters we have stored in boxes in our closets from thousands of other unlucky parents must be a small aberration.

Fortunately, what happened to us was slight. Alec

never was put in Special Education classes, he was never labeled (except once, ludicrously and incorrectly by a medical clinic that admitted finally it had made a mistake), and he found the love, comfort, and support of a small private school where he is growing to adulthood now with high hopes.

This book remains angry, but we end our personal story and turn to other cases, what other people are saying about mislabeling of kids and what parents can do for their own kids. There are specific things that can help kids and special groups set up for that purpose, and we name them. There are other sources, and a parent has to take the time to find them. The time of a child's learning is so very brief and then it is gone and it can never be found again.

We tell you two last stories about Alec, a normal little ten-year-old boy in a loving school, realizing something new about his world every day. Perhaps he is a little scarred by what happened to him; perhaps it has made him stronger.

When he was eight and had taken piano lessons for a year, he prepared for his first class recital. One afternoon, he sat down at the piano and wrote a line of music. It is not so very much. The line of music rises and then trails off because it is unfinished—as he is unfinished. It is a line of great expectations and the first song he ever wrote. The notes in the line rise, then fall, then wait on the edge at the end of the line for the next line to begin.

When he was just eight years old, he explained time to his father. It was a beautiful spring day and he said, "Look, Dad."

"What?"

"The buds are on the trees. See? All the buds go up and down the branches. The buds grow and grow. Then they become—what? What happens to them?"

"Leaves," said Dad.

"You're right," said the little teacher. "And the grass gets green and then it's summer."

"Right," said the student.

"And then, the leaves get red and they get on the ground and then it's fall." Alec paused and smiled. "And then it gets all snow again and then it's—guess what?"

"Winter," said Dad.

"You're right again," said the little teacher. He was so proud of his dad. The seasons come and go and are gone so quickly and then the cycle begins again.

Alec is in spring. His song is just beginning and it is not going to be finished for a long time.

PART TWO

Nothing Special

6

The Silver
Lining

Special Education came out of a good concern. Before the
1970s, there was plenty of evidence that children who ran
afoul of a cross teacher or who were a discipline problem
were being denied an education. They were expelled from
the school system and there was no appeal. This made
some people angry.

The Children's Defense Fund was one such group.
Based in Washington, D.C., it commissioned a survey and
concluded in 1972 that about 8 million school-age children
were not in school.[1]

The reasons were many, but in a large number of cases
the defense fund found the children were simply handicapped and the schools either could not—or some teachers
did not want to—deal with this. For instance, the defense
fund discovered that it was a common policy of schools to

tell parents of children in wheelchairs or children suffering from cerebral palsy that the school simply had no place for such children and they were better off at home.

Another group of children denied access to a public education were the growing numbers of pregnant teenagers. But by far the largest group of children forced out of school were those considered behavioral problems. If you made trouble in school, you were expelled. It had always been that way; it seemed it would always be that way. Except the times suddenly changed.

The political and social rhetoric of the 1960s spoke of equality of opportunity in all areas and the need to bring racial minorities into the mainstream of white culture. The discoveries of groups like the Children's Defense Fund fit in with this social movement. One of their discoveries was key: In every region and in every age group, black children were several times more likely than white kids to be out of school.[2]

So the argument ran: What good was it to improve the racial content of textbooks (a movement of the 1960s in education) and develop new curricula on such subjects as black history, if hundreds of thousands of black kids were outside the schoolhouse door? Could we allow the public school system to continue to refuse to serve so many children?

This kind of reasoning led eventually to Congressional action. In 1975, Congress passed Education for All Handicapped Act, Public Law 94-142. The act states simply that the states must provide a free and appropriate education for all students. Period.

Unfortunately, no one since has ever decided what Congress meant when it used the word *appropriate* in the law. Does *appropriate* mean effective? Does it mean that every student should be taught to read and write and count?

Educators have shuddered at that interpretation and education associations and unions as well as school districts have fought in the courts against those demanding an accounting of how kids come up short despite ten or twelve years of public schooling.

The courts have sided with the educators. With a few narrow exceptions, parents have lost cases when they argue that their child has been victimized by "educational malpractice"; courts are not willing to get into arguments about what constitutes effective education.

As a result, of course, our public school system continues to erode. Millions of mostly white, mostly middle-class parents—and their children—vote with their feet on the effectiveness of the school systems. They opt for private schools, whatever the cost. In too many cities private education is booming and public education has become a ghetto for the neglected.

Among the children called handicapped under PL 94-142, by the way, are the gifted. This strange inclusion underscores the fact that "fitting in at school" has become the new criterion of handicap. Yet programs for the gifted are minuscule compared to those for the children that schools decide are deficient.

One aspect of PL 94-142 established as a matter of law the existence of a new disease—learning disabilities.

Learning disabilities came out of the truth of American education—kids were failing to keep up with their European and Japanese counterparts in almost every area of study. Declining test scores were reported routinely.

Who was to blame? You had only two choices: Blame the schools and teachers, or blame the students and parents.

Educators and psychologists—many supported by government grants—naturally focused on the students as the cause of declining test scores. It came as no surprise that they discovered that the American student was a sicky, and those bad test results were not caused by bad teachers, bad curricula, bad textbooks, or by a rotted, racist public school system.

In large part, parents accepted the fact that the problem of the schools came from their kids and not from anything wrong with the schools.

Ernest Mueller, superintendent of the Oak Park (Illinois) public school system, told us: "We've done such a good selling job on parents that it's hard to get away from it. If you try to cut down on Special Ed, you get parents upset. No matter how much evidence you can put in front of them that labeling and separating children is harmful, they still want it."

Special Education—and PL 94-142—came along at the right time to save public education. School enrollment was in steep decline in the early 1970s. This meant that there was a glut of teachers on the market, there were too many school buildings, and school budgets were under sharp local voter scrutiny. Two educators wrote a gleeful essay, laying out how Special Education under the new law was "the silver lining in the cloud" of declining enrollments.[3]

Expanding Special Education would let school districts hang on to redundant teachers and administrators—and even hire more. It would find uses for those empty school buildings.

Between 1970 and 1974, enrollment declined all over the country, with student counts in the elementary and secondary public schools tumbling. But even in the face of this decline, many states found a way not only to retain teachers, but actually hire more! In Illinois, for example, which lost 2.9 percent of its enrollment, the number of special teachers and support staff jumped 61.5 percent during that period![4]

Persuade parents a child was mentally "sick" and you could justify putting him in his own class with a few others who were also sick. You could hire "resource help" to work with him "one on one." And what Scrooge could object to spending more money on sick kids?

The effects of PL 94-142 went into full operation in 1978. The change in the educational scenery has been startling in these past eight years. Take a look: In 1970, 6 percent of all children were in Special Education programs. Since then, raw numbers of school enrollment have declined by about 4 million. Sixteen years later, in 1986, the number in Special Education classes hovered over 11 percent, taking in more than 4 million of our children.[5]

In other words, we had fewer kids in school in those sixteen years—but more of them were suddenly in Special Education programs, which required more teachers, more support staff, new school buildings, new busing contracts, special supplies.

Eleven percent is a national figure. In some states it is much higher, in other states, much lower. For example: Massachusetts has 15 percent in Special Education; Colorado has 8 percent. Statistically, this swing doesn't make a lot of sense.

Where had all these sick children come from?

The biggest single chunk of them came under the heading of "learning-disabled," a pseudo-disease that had not even existed in 1970. LD—and it is a label just like retarded or crippled—suddenly became the most fashionable disease in education. More kids were assigned the LD disease than were in speech therapy. And the push was on by experts in the education field to up the figures even more dramatically—one suggested up to 30 percent of our kids were victims of LD and ought to be segregated in part- or full-time special programs. Thirty percent!

How did all of these kids get sick so fast? One argument from the educators goes this way: More kids are surviving childhood diseases that used to wipe out weak kids with sick brains. Maybe they walk and talk and look normal, but they have subtle brain damage and it only shows up when they go to school and get the expert diagnosis of a teacher. The fact that this theory has never been seriously researched or demonstrated to be true does not stop many teachers from throwing it out as an explanation for all these "special" kids.

A second argument goes this way: The world has become a dangerous place, full of nuclear wastes, illegal dumps, tainted water tables. No one can argue with that. Naturally, kids born in such a world are more defective than children of an earlier generation born in an unpolluted world. Their parents don't see the differences, the pediatricians can't spot defects, aunts and uncles don't see them either—but put such a child in class with *normal* children, and we can depend on a teacher to spot the brain damage.

One eye specialist who pooh-poohs this so-far-unsupported-by-research argument said talk about brain damage and brain defects is only speculation, part of what he calls the 1953 Chevy explanation.

What is the 1953 Chevy explanation? It is answered with a question: Did you walk near a 1953 Chevy when you were pregnant with Johnny?

Yes, I did.

There. That explains why Johnny can't read in school.

At this point, some readers might think we are in the realm of Wonderland. We are—but it is terribly real. In 1983, a University of California study concluded that the proportion of "defective" children born in the United States has nearly doubled in twenty-five years.[6]

What led to this startling and frightening conclusion? The learned study factored in heavily statistical reports of children diagnosed as having learning disabilities, which was not even a disease twenty-five years ago and which many doubt has much validity now.

The researchers at the University of California warned that the full extent of new "defects" could not be known until babies reached fourth grade and teachers had a fair chance of diagnosing learning disabilities!

Teachers were suddenly cited as medical experts and a new disease was spread in the land, whose existence is totally dependent on a teacher's subjective judgment. And that disease was lumped in with routine medical statistics on such diseases as chronic bronchitis and diagnoses of orthopedic problems by medical professionals.

In other words: Alice has a broken arm and is diagnosed by a doctor after X rays, and the arm is set. Adam has trouble reading and his teacher concludes he is learning-disabled. He is shunted off to Special Education classes. The California study concludes both diagnoses are valid and are part of proving that more kids are defective than ever before.

The law passed in 1975 has clearly been misused by researchers, school systems, teachers, and the psychology branch of medical science to inflate an education system that was leaking enrollment, money, and influence—not to mention tenured teachers' jobs.

If the increased number of kids in Special Education programs is not the fault of the parents or children—in other words, if there really isn't a large and growing number of weird kids in the world, and the educators have not proved there is—could the fault lie with the teaching profession allied with a psychological brotherhood of rubber-stampers?

Examinations of the deep and abiding ills in the professions of psychology and psychiatry have been made elsewhere. Psychiatry has been routinely used in countries such as the Soviet Union to label dissidents as "insane" and subject them to barbaric "treatment" by doctors who have long been willing to sell their professional ethics for survival.

Last year, psychologists and psychiatrists held a meeting to agree on a new dictionary of psychological terms and to invest old diseases with new meanings. Is there such a mental disease as "masochism"? Feminist psychologists said no, others said yes—according to their political views. They threw out some old diseases and invented some new ones—rather in the manner of a group of people deciding which restaurant to have lunch at, one psychologist remarked.

The willingness of psychologists to depend on outmoded—even false—data, to change nomenclature depending on what pressure group is demanding it, and, above all, to misdiagnose and then say that misdiagnosis is part of the routine of psychological testing makes their judgments suspect in areas beyond education.

In court cases, for example, in which the defense argues the accused was insane at the time of a crime, it is commonplace for the prosecution and then the defense to each present a parcel of "expert witnesses" from the ranks of the psychology profession, all of whom have examined the accused and all of whom are quite willing to reach wildly different diagnoses of his mental state at the time of a crime committed months or years before. Psychology is a study of the mind, but the professionals in the field act as if the study and the theories have long ago reached concrete conclusions.

A teacher's recommendation for psychological testing is a challenge to too many psychologists to "find something wrong with the child." The criteria of what is normal and what is not changes from child to child, and from psychologist to psychologist. Parents are whipsawed between the school and the psychological testing center, are buried under a blizzard of bogus terms, and, finally, are forced to give up the fight for their child's rights because too many expert witnesses are arrayed against them. It is a shame— but it is certainly not science.

Ignoring psychology and psychologists for the moment, let us look at the American teacher and the American school. The teacher sees herself today as embattled, and the image she draws of the school and her classroom is inevitably drawn from the image of the inner-city ghetto. In pleasant suburban towns across the country, in white, middle-class communities whose only black faces belong to maids and butlers, the teacher still uses the jargon of race, of inner city, of an unstable, chaotic America to describe herself, her surroundings, her students, and her profession. If you doubt it, don't talk to teachers, listen to them talk among themselves, as they agree that the breakup of the family is hurting them in the classroom, that today's kids are street-smart wiseguys, that parents are the problem standing in the way of a solution, that kids don't respect teachers as they believe teachers were respected in an earlier, bucolic era.

We lived in a such a suburb for a long time and when we dealt with the local, all-white public school, we were astonished to find a full-time social worker on the staff. Why would a social worker be employed in a suburb with strong churches, notable family life (largely Catholic, mostly ethnic Irish and Italian), relatively high income, and very few instances of "broken homes"? Because school professionals see their job in the rhetoric and conflicts described by the black inner city.

One mother who lived in an affluent suburb of a large city told us she was visited by a social worker sent from the school. The social worker had been consulting with the child, who had been diagnosed as retarded by the school professionals. (The school district was later forced to admit that it had misdiagnosed the boy.) The social worker said that as part of the child's "individualized educational program," he was required to make "home visits" and the mother was required to open her home to him.

The social worker came to the house, walked into the kitchen, and said: "Washed the floor for me, right? I'm sure you don't keep it this clean all the time."

This insulting remark is not uncommon in the profession of social work, as honest social workers will agree. Two generations of dealing with mostly black clients in the inner city—clients who cannot refuse their ministrations—have infected social workers with a disease of arrogance, cynicism, and distrust of the client families they service. White parents are only now beginning to feel some of the professional contempt that black parents have long grown accustomed to. The woman in the affluent suburb was so angered by that visit that she fought back—but the battle continues on other fronts every day of the year.

The contempt for clients pervades the social work profession, and it spills into the teaching ranks as well. Read any large newspaper with a letters-to-the-editor column and look for letters from teachers defending their profession. The letters have a common theme: Children don't learn because they are not good material—there is something wrong with the quality of their brains or their parents —or they watch too much television, or they have learning disabilities and low IQ scores, or they aren't properly "socialized," or they have emotional problems. "We have to take everyone," is the common lament of public school teachers.

In our studies of Special Education, we reached the conclusion that the system is used in many areas of the country to discriminate against black children—to force black kids into "special" schools in large numbers so that the old segregation pattern struck down in 1954 in *Brown v. Board of Education* is repeated . . . for the good of the child.

A larger percentage of black children is in Special Education in the United States than white children. Though black children make up only 16 percent of the school population, they make up nearly 40 percent of the classes for so-called educable mentally retarded children. The teachers accept the figures but say it is not racism on their part, nor is it the fault of the tests; it is just a thing they would rather not talk about.[7]

What they would rather not talk about is this: Many teachers believe more blacks are in Special Education because blacks are inherently inferior. Blacks became inferior through poor diet, eating junk food, living junk lives. Joan Beck, an oft-cited educational writer and advocate of early childhood education, has suggested that the unstimulating environment of inner-city blacks actually causes neurological defects—about the wildest theory to come along since Dr. Alvin Shockley said black brains were inferior to white brains.

The whole movement toward earlier and earlier education programs—start kids in school at two or three— suggests that earlier diagnosis of childhood ills will help weed out kids who need help, and they will be dealt with.

In Los Angeles, black Mayor Thomas Bradley has suggested that it might be in the best interest of some black children to be taken away from their parents so that they could learn a better sense of values to deal with modern society. Blithely ignored is the fact that any sort of testing of children at early ages is difficult and remarkably unreliable, even when well done, even when done to spot physical problems. Ignored is the proposition that most children aren't ready for separation from their families at such early ages. Most ignored is the fact that current remedial techniques rarely result in much improvement, even in good programs.

Who will decide which families are worthy of being left alone and which families must be broken up, for the good of the child? Big Brother slouches closer to reality in education and Special Ed than in any other area affecting family life and individual rights.

Experiments in manipulating family life have gone on for a generation among welfare families—mostly black, mostly in big cities—and now the experiment is spreading to whites, to the suburbs, to small towns.

The attack on the family deflects attention from a close examination of how the schools continue to fail generation after generation of students, special or not. Johnny could not read thirty years ago in Rudolf Flesch's landmark work, and he still can't read. Ignorance feeds on ignorance, as new teachers—raised in the television generation—replace the last teachers who ever had to learn anything. And it is not the fault of the school. It is never the fault of the school.

The social worker who visited the affluent mother and asked her about her clean floors also delivered this bit of educationist wisdom: "Seeing a social worker would be helpful for every family."

It gives us all something to look forward to.

7

Where Intelligence Came From

Schools have provided special classes for children labeled as retarded for nearly a century.

Does everyone know what *retarded* means?

Retarded covers a broad range, from adults who can't make change for a dollar to children who can't control their bowel functions at the age of ten.

Retarded is one of the great catchall words that mean exactly what the speaker wants them to mean. Humpty Dumpty in *Through the Looking Glass* could not have put it better.

Some define *retardation* in the way that a Supreme Court justice once defined the idea of pornography: "I don't know what it is exactly, but I know it when I see it."

Few parents know that retardation is not a disease at all. Retarded children can become retarded because of other diseases or accidents—but retardation is merely a score on a test. It is not a disease in itself, but a symptom of some other problem, and the degree of retardation is defined by a score on a written test. Keep that in mind: *Degree of retardation turns out to be nothing but a score on a test.* The problem underlying the retardation may be curable— and it may not. Unfortunately, Special Education focuses on the symptom rather than on the underlying problem.

The test score most used in American education is the score on one of several widely used IQ tests. Everyone knows about the friendly IQ test. Everyone knows that IQ is something you have to a greater or lesser extent. It is a miracle of modern science that quantifies all our capacity for intelligence in a single number. Get much above 100— the absolute even number in which a person's mental age equals his chronological age—and you have "gifted" people of superior intelligence. Get below that number, and you have various degrees of people with less and less intellectual capacity.

The test is an attempt—a feeble and rather fraudulent attempt as you will see—to measure intelligence by asking a few questions, then assigning a mental age to the child being tested. It was developed in 1904 by Alfred Binet (pronounced Bin-AY), who had been commissioned by the French government to find a way to identify children in need of help in the schools. (As a side note: About a third of all French children in school today are assigned to special low-track courses. The courses effectively isolate and hold back children from reaching for the top rung of starter jobs in French government and business.)

Binet, a French psychologist, was a careful and introspective man, who had spent the last years of the nineteenth century trying to prove the widely believed theory that the size of a person's skull could reveal how much intelligence was contained in his brain. Binet concluded at last that the idea of brain size equaling intelligence was wrong, and he turned to other methods of probing the extent of intelligence.

He devised the IQ test as a series of questions and

tasks, graded in difficulty according to the age of the average child presumed to be able to accomplish them. The child proceeded through the tasks until he could no longer do them. At that point, his mental age was pronounced, and if it was markedly lower than his chronological age, he was marked out for special work.

At first, Binet merely subtracted the mental age from the chronological age, but this was thought too imprecise. Binet had in mind the idea that one's upward progress in education was a matter of "catching up" with the norm. It can be supposed in reading Binet's work that he really meant the IQ test to be a temporary, helpful, interim measure to aid teachers in pinpointing a child's problems and then attacking them, so that the child could return as quickly as possible to the ranks of the "normal."

Binet's grading was not good enough. After all, a four-year-old child with a mental age of two had more serious intelligence problems than a sixteen-year-old with a mental age of fourteen. The problem was solved in 1912—a year after Binet's early death—by German psychologist W. Stern. He invented the idea of dividing the chronological age by the mental age (as registered on the tests) to come up with the norm. The norm was 100, in which the age of the test-taker exactly corresponded to the mental age, as determined by the results of the test. (Of course, this is nonsense. No one has devised a test yet of what a forty-two-year-old man should be able to do. What is a forty-two-year-old man's mental age? If it turns out to be twelve, then the man drops into the category of a moron—which is reasonable if he still believes in the validity of IQ tests at the age of forty-two.)

It is important to see how the IQ test has changed in value since Binet's experiments. Binet himself never claimed he was measuring some fixed, inborn trait that amounted to mental horsepower. He believed, in fact, in changing one's intelligence quotient through mental calisthenics that would get children off the rolls of the retarded.

He also protested the idea that his test could be used to rank all children on a single scale to define the quality of their minds. He said that would be a dangerous use of his test. "The scale," he wrote in 1905, "properly speaking, does not permit the measure of the intelligence, because intellectual qualities are not superposable, and therefore cannot be measured as linear surfaces are measured."[1]

Of course, what Binet warned against is exactly what has come to pass. The IQ test in the United States has always been used to measure literally a fixed idea of intelligence. That intelligence cannot be measured in this way does not stop testers from doing so in millions of tests given every year.

Binet was terribly afraid his methods might be used by teachers and bureaucrats to justify creating "self-fulfilling prophecies" in children they wanted to judge as inadequate. "It is really too easy to discover signs of backwardness in an individual when one is forewarned," he said. "This would be to operate as the graphologists did who, when Dreyfus was believed to be guilty, discovered in his handwriting signs of a traitor or spy."[2] (The case of Alfred Dreyfus, a French army officer accused of being a traitor, finally was resolved by discovering he was innocent. The pseudoscience of graphoanalysis—cited earlier—continues to fascinate the teaching profession as a clue to a child's intelligence and inner thoughts. "Coloring within the lines" and "scientific" interpretation of a child's drawings are cousins to graphoanalysis.)

Binet seemed to know he had invented a monster that would be uncaged after his death. "It will never be to one's credit to have attended a special school. We should at the least spare from this mark those who do not deserve it. Mistakes are excusable, especially at the beginning. But if they become too gross, they could injure the reputation of these new institutions."[3]

So what is intelligence, anyway, since it is the base of labeling so many millions of children residing in Special

Education classes today? At a child-guidance clinic in a Chicago suburb, a tester and evaluator said blithely that IQ is "like a gas gauge. It tells you whether the tank is half-empty or half-full."

Nonsense. The IQ test is a bit of a fraud, and even a leader in the educational use of such tests to label kids admitted it once. Psychologist E. G. Boring allowed that "intelligence is what intelligence tests measure," but he went on to push for their widespread use in the school.

The only thing anyone agrees on about IQ tests is that kids with higher IQs do better in school—as a rule—than kids with lower IQs, though the differences between someone with 110 IQ and a 99 IQ, for example, might be nil.

Of course, since the IQ test has been shoveled together over the years, there is a strong suspicion that the test itself is nothing but schoolwork focused in microcosm, and that intelligent children unfamiliar with a particular societal setting—say, black city kids thrust into the countryside—might do worse than kids already there.

The IQ test is rigorously defended in American society as an absolute judge of intelligence, and parents have tended not to question its validity—even though the founder of the IQ test had more than a few questions. Of course, IQ tests must call the same children stupid that the teachers do. The IQ test would not be any use if the kids it called stupid succeeded in school and the high scorers did not. So the IQ testers, over the years, have chopped and changed the scale to coincide with teachers' judgments.

Binet's little invention was an idea whose time had come. It was taken up with enthusiasm across the channel in England, where Charles Spearman developed the factor analysis—which has become a foundation of modern social science statistics—to study IQ. Working along similar lines was Cyril Burt, an incredible humbug, who studied intelligence in a number of twins raised separately to see if they developed the same IQ scores.

Burt was a gem. His great work concluded that intelligence was fixed and hereditary, because the twins all came out with similar IQ scores despite having been raised in different environments and given different educations. His results marked a milestone in psychological testing. Just about every psychology text in use in America through the late 1970s cited the Burt study as one of the pillars of psychological testing. The only problem was that the Burt study was a total fraud.

Somebody somewhere along the line should have gotten suspicious. Burt never even identified the IQ test he had supposedly given to thousands of pairs of relatives. Many of his papers made no attempt to follow normal scientific reporting procedure; no specifics were given about how or when the data had been collected. Yet they were published in scientific journals and widely quoted all over the world. Why?

The inescapable conclusion is that Burt's ideas of hereditary intelligence were simply convenient for a lot of the people involved. Though Burt gave so little information about how he reached his conclusions, IQ correlations were reported as sober scientific fact and given to three decimal places! In fact, that was how Burt's fraud was discovered. Various researchers became interested in the fact that IQ correlations in Burt's study remained identical—to three decimal places—even when the number of cases he claimed to have studied increased dramatically over the years. This, the researchers knew, was simply impossible.

In 1976, a writer for the London *Sunday Times* decided to try to find two research assistants Burt had described as giving many of the tests on which he based his conclusions. It turned out they didn't exist. Burt's co-workers had never met them. When Burt was asked about them, he replied that they had immigrated to Australia or New Zealand— and the date he gave for their immigration actually preceded the time, according to his published papers, that they were busily working at giving IQ tests to twins!

(Some psychologists to this day still argue that intelligence is fixed and hereditary, and that if Burt had really done his study instead of faking it, the results would have been the same.)

Binet's probings into the idea of intelligence became deadly serious in America about the time of World War I. A man named H. H. Goddard was the director of the Vineland Training School for Feeble Minded Boys and Girls in New Jersey. Goddard is one of the gods of American educational psychology and his rearrangement of the American IQ test—based on Binet's early work—is standard today.

Goddard did not see the IQ test as roughly measuring the ability of children to perform certain tasks at a given time up to their chronological age level. He saw intelligence testing as a golden chain, stretching through the ranks of mankind from top to bottom, linking us all together in fixed positions on a scale.

The IQ tests could measure the lowest end of the intellectual ladder. Goddard called these people "primitive idiots." The category has now been softened to "profoundly retarded."

Next up the scale were the imbeciles (now called trainable mentally handicapped or trainable mentally retarded). They are children who score between 40 and 55 on an IQ examination.

Above the imbeciles in Goddard's divine scheme was the moron (today called the educable mentally retarded or handicapped). These children score between 55 and 70 on the test.

Above the moron was the normal child. And above the normal was the gifted, those who exceeded in intelligence their chronological age, such as the women of the upper-IQ club called MENSA, who posed half-naked last year in a special section for *Playboy* magazine called "The Women of MENSA." Their intelligence level was written all over their faces.

Goddard, among his many contributions to psychology, did a wonderful case study of the Kallikak family. He traced this family through its personal history and he concluded that defective intelligence was passed on like a bad penny from generation to generation; it was definitely inherited.

Goddard's pioneering work and that of other IQ testers pushed Congress to enact a number of strict immigration laws to halt the flood of "defective" foreigners, such as those from Eastern Europe who were clamoring to our shores. And the American South enthusiastically adopted the principle that mental defects are passed from generation to generation, and a series of laws calling for forced sterilization of people judged mentally deficient were enacted. Such sterilization—primarily of black girls—continued in parts of the South until the last decade.

Stephen Jay Gould, the eminently readable natural historian, traces the history of how IQ tests, phrenology, craniometry, and other frauds have been misused to prejudice findings against people we want to find something against. In his book *The Mismeasure of Man*, he notes that Goddard faked most of the data on the Kallikak family and that the theory of hereditary IQ is not only unproven but actually unprovable, since it is based on faulty reasoning from beginning to end.

Goddard, when not wreaking havoc in one area, slammed into education. He established the tradition that some of his assistants could unerringly recognize the mentally deficient even without giving them the IQ test. The IQ test could be given merely to back up the judgment of an assistant.

That is the way it is largely used today in schools. A teacher decides a child is retarded; the psychotesters respectfully listen to her judgment, give the child a test, and, lo and behold!, they prove she was right. That proves, they say, that teachers *know* children. Others who have looked at the process see it differently. It proves only that psychotesting is an expensive rubber stamp.

This very American idea that intelligence was fixed and

hereditary, and there was not much you could do about it, appealed to those in the education profession—as well as certain government bureaucracies.

Lewis Terman became a true pioneer of the modern commercial psychometric test industry. He revised Binet's test and popularized it. He was a very certain man, very precise, a great believer in the IQ test. He believed that eventually the country would be rationally governed by technicians skilled in the application of such tests. People would be allocated to their proper calling in life according to their tested mental capacity.

Terman even knew how much intelligence you needed for various professions. For example, he wrote, "Anything above 85 IQ in the case of a barber probably represents so much dead waste."[4]

Terman absolutely rejected Binet's idea of training minds to improve them once the IQ tests showed some sort of lack of learning. You couldn't improve what wasn't there, according to Terman; intelligence was fixed and innate.

He developed what has come to be called the Stanford-Binet test for IQ. It is Holy Writ in the education field. Terman believed that IQ test results should be used to push children with inadequate brains into lesser education "tracks" in schools, or even into nonacademic education. He did not believe anyone should fool themselves by believing that hard work and aspirations might lead some underachievers to become successful.

Terman's views—and those of Goddard—have prevailed in American education, and not Binet's cautious experimentation and his warnings that his invention could be misused.

The IQ test idea was given a boost in World War I by a Harvard researcher named Robert M. Yerkes, who talked the U.S. Army into allowing him to give group IQ tests to soldiers on the theory that it would help identify officer material. The tests were wonderful and were cited for decades by academics of all stripes as showing the sorry state of American intelligence and why it wasn't the fault of schools or teachers that Johnny couldn't read (Johnny has been having reading problems for a long time now).

Yerkes gave two versions of his test—the Alpha for those who could read, and the Beta for illiterates in the army. He concluded that the average white American adult male was little more than a moron, with a mental age slightly over thirteen.

He had all sorts of wonderful subcategories. The average male of Polish descent had a mental age of 10.74, and that made him the dumbest of all the European immigrant groups. Of course, Yerkes was not surprised to learn that blacks were at the mental bottom, with a mental age of only 10.41.

Out of Yerkes's nonsense came the Army Alpha test, which is the great-ancestor of all written, group-administered intelligence tests. The test you took in grammar school or in the army, filled with analogies or number-sequence problems, is the descendant of the Yerkes test.

When the Yerkes statistics were published, there were some who protested. One was the young journalist Walter Lippmann, who wrote a series of essays in *The New Republic* criticizing the tests. He wrote of his fear that they would be used to label children as inferior at the outset of their schooling.

Terman wrote a reply. As all psychotesters were to do when faced with a disagreement, he argued that Lippmann's views reflected "problems" in his own mind.

"Mr. Lippmann does not charge that the tests have been thus abused, but that they easily could be," he wrote. "Very true; but they simply aren't. That is one of the recognized rules of the game. Isn't it funny what horrible possibilities an excited brain can conjure up?"[5]

Today, teachers pepper their conversation with talk about "slow learners," "borderline retards," or "gifted" children—solely on the basis of the IQ scores they have in their files. One teacher told us of a colleague in the system who was so determined to teach only "high-quality" students that at the beginning of each year he checked all their IQ scores and found a way to transfer out of his class any student who scored below a high-quality IQ cutoff.

The silliness of fixed IQ scores is perpetuated at every level of education. Larry Foster, director of the Proviso Area Exceptional Children Special Education district near Chicago, said, "A kid with an eighty-five IQ level can't succeed in a normal class without help." Such a flat statement by someone in such a high position gives one pause —until one considers that most states, including Illinois, and such groups as the American Association of Mental Deficiency regard an 85 IQ as a normal IQ score. A thing means exactly what I want it to mean, no more and no less. A lot of people in Special Education today would certainly agree with Humpty Dumpty.

The IQ test has come to be used as a bludgeon in the hands of various teachers and various school authorities with various ideas of how to use it. The bewildered parents are no match for pseudoexperts spouting pseudoscientific garbage and citing past studies that, more often than not, turn out to have been frauds perpetrated by humbuggers without an ounce of compunction.

"But the IQ test is only one of many tools we have to determine a child's intelligence." This is the whiny reply of many educators, psychologists, and paraprofessional testers. What they are saying in that self-revealing statement is that perhaps the IQ test is wrong, the result is wrong, it is interpreted wrongly—but it is only one of the wrong things we have at our disposal. Because—make no mistake about it—based on bad assumptions as it is, the IQ test is indeed the best tool the educators have on hand. Their other tests and tools are, when not directly derived from the IQ test, more often than not simply ways to make subjective judgments sound scientific. Educators know this and admit it among themselves. In a 1984 pamphlet the Illinois State

Board of Education sent out to principals, five of their experts wrote:

> The whole area of intellectual functioning is one which we are not very good at understanding, let alone measuring. We cannot see or otherwise demonstrate the presence of a problem—all we can see is certain behaviors in the child which we *assume* to come from various sources, possibly chemical, possibly neurological, possibly emotional, but which neither medical science nor education is able to prove or even define clearly. These assumptions are conjectures—observing certain behaviors, we suggest a possible cause which would link them, but we cannot prove these conjectures and certainly have no really reliable tests of them.[6]

An IQ test is just a test, nothing more or less. It is a fallible and fragile instrument of measurement—rather like a carpenter using his thumb and a good eye to predict the opening needed for a door he hasn't built yet.

Many things can produce a low IQ score that have nothing to do with a child's potential. He might be anxious about tests in general. He might be sick or tired on test day. He might have poor eye-hand coordination caused by an undiscovered eye problem. He might have language difficulties—some bright kids speak appalling English and some bright immigrant children are still struggling with the American tongue when it comes time to give them IQ tests. The tests assume familiarity with cultural expressions that all children may not know. A child may be bullied at the time of testing by the tester who wants the results to come out the way he predicts they should come out.

And so, in third grade or fourth, a child is given his IQ number, which also identifies his seat on the education bus.

Tell this to educators and they listen and nod patronizingly and say there are always abuses in systems and, well, it's the only measure we have.

Why defend a testing procedure that has a history of prejudice, racism, misuse, and fraud? Because if a child is not intelligent, the school and the teacher are off the hook. They really don't have to accept the blame for not getting Johnny to read.

And the IQ number is so . . . so real. It satisfies the American need for social elitism. And since everyone uses it, it must be right.

So Johnny and Jennifer answer some questions wrong one day in a classroom at the beginning of their education and they begin the one-way railroad ride to the Special Education dumping ground.

8

Emotions

Special Education in America has a full plate. Not only does it seek to include children of lesser intelligence in its ranks —no matter how fraudulent the history of testing and questionable the diagnoses—it reaches for more.

And more comes from an amorphous category of kids called "emotionally disturbed." You might suspect this catchall phrase is a growth industry in American education. You'd be right.

In 1970, there were 113,000 children labeled as emotionally disturbed. A decade passed and enrollment in school declined dramatically. In 1980, there were 352,000 children called emotionally disturbed.[1] But the figure isn't high enough. Some education experts say that under various guidelines used by school districts to describe emotionally disturbed children, up to 30 percent of all kids in school would fit the category! Obviously, it is getting easier for a kid to get an emotionally disturbed label pinned on him.

(To categorize a child as emotionally disturbed does not even require the fraudulent test procedures used to snare so-called mentally handicapped kids into the Special Education trap. Most identification of emotionally disturbed children comes from teachers.

In fact, one textbook on such children states that "in the final analysis, there are no adequate instruments for measuring emotional disturbance and . . . identification of disturbed children depends on subjective judgments."[2]

So who are the emotionally disturbed? The ones identified by the teachers. They are the ones who talk too much out of turn in class. They are the ones who grab other kids, who won't do what they are told (according to the teacher), who do "bizarre" (a current favorite teacher word) things to attract attention.

They are the class cutups and class clowns. Quiet children rarely attract the sort of notice that will slate them for a one-way trip into the emotionally disturbed classification. If they get into trouble and into Special Ed, they wind up in the retarded grouping.

Are parents told that diagnoses of emotional disturbances are so subjective? Of course not. Instead, the kids are put through a battery of pseudoscientific tests that go under names like projective tests, word-association tests, draw-your-family tests, personality-inventory examinations. When it comes time then to send Johnny or Alice into Special Education—where his or her emotional problem will presumably be worked out—the talk to convince parents to go along is all about what the test results show.

The tests described are based on one idea: that children are unable or unwilling to communicate directly (according to the authority making this judgment) and that their innermost thoughts can be revealed by trick tests. That is the idea behind the famous inkblot test developed by Rorschach. It is a projective test in which the secret thoughts and emotional state of the person being tested can be interpreted by a trained professional reading what the person thinks a blob of ink looks like.

In children, the main such "test" used is an analysis of their drawings or their handwriting. Parents have told us that their children were judged depressed because they used black or purple crayons to make a picture—when the simple truth was that the black and purple crayons were the only ones not broken in the box or the only ones left when the child was allowed to choose!

One mother wrote that her child was deemed profoundly angry when he drew a picture of himself colored in orange. Orange is an angry color. It was also the color of the uniform of the school's baseball team—to which the child belonged.

There is enough guilt in these pseudoscientific tests for parents. It is not unusual for the tester to point out that the child is severely disturbed because parents have pressured him or her to be normal—when it was very possible the child would be happier in a more retarded state! This sort of mumbo jumbo can be very frightening to parents (and imagine how much more frightening to a little boy or girl asked to perform nonsensical tests).

Are there emotionally disturbed children? Are there children, as there are adults, who are anxious, fearful, overwhelmed by the stresses of their lives? No doubt. But are such children identified and helped by school personnel? The evidence says the process by which such children are diagnosed is haphazard and fraudulent—and that the treatments they get in schools actually compound their problems.

What educators mean by emotional disturbance is behavior that displeases someone in authority. They know nothing about the inner emotional state of a child—how could they?

What really makes a child behave oddly is of no interest to educators, even though there is plenty of evidence that a child's "abnormal" behavior may well be a quite reasonable reaction to a problem in the way his eyes or ears are letting him perceive the world—or to a rigid school system that ruthlessly punishes any individual who does not immediately "fit in."

Signs of emotional disturbance are all over the ball-park in education—kids who whisper and pass notes in class when they should be quiet can be emotionally disturbed, as well as children who barricade themselves in the hall closet. Naturally, the place for such a child is Special Education. No one quite knows why, however. It is just a way of getting rid of the child—which is what Special Education classrooms and facilities are used for more and more. The dumping ground, the garbage heap at the back of education's shining front, Special Education is not nearly as special as people say it is.

A parent, told his child is retarded, can blame God Parents of disturbed children are urged by the educators to blame themselves. There is probably not a child on Earth who could not be called emotionally disturbed at some point in his life by some educator's criterion.

In our case, our son was described as passive, anxious, and fearful because an examiner said he had insisted his mother be present at a test. The truth was different—the examiner conveniently forgot he had asked the mother to be present at the test!

Another mother said anxiety mounted in her son during his testing for emotional disturbance. "They had him so frightened he was under the table, and then they said to me, 'See? He's under the table. That's disturbed behavior.' But he never acted like that before."

Dr. Thomas Szasz, professor of psychiatry at the State University of New York (Syracuse), has earned the wrath of the psychological testers with his long-time criticism of institutional psychodiagnosis. Here is Dr. Szasz's careful argument against such testing and such test results. More parents should be aware of them.

I have discussed and documented elsewhere that there is no behavior or person that a modern psychiatrist cannot plausibly diagnose as abnormal or ill.

Instead of belaboring this subject, I shall cite a set of guidelines—conforming closely to the rule, "Heads I win, tails you lose"—offered by a psychiatrist for finding psychiatric problems in school children. In a paper advocating psychiatric services in public schools, the author lists the following types of behavior as "symptomatic of deeper underlying disturbances. . . ."

He goes on to list the emotional disturbances. Does your child qualify in one of these categories?

1. Academic problems such as an underachiever, overachiever, erratic, uneven performance in school work.

2. Social problems with siblings, with peers, such as an aggressive child, a submissive child, a showoff.

3. Oddities in relations with parents or other authority figures defined as defiant behavior at times, submissive behavior, trying to ingratiate himself with authority figures.

4. Any overt "behavioral manifestation" such as tics, nail-biting, thumb-sucking, and *interests more befitting to the opposite sex (such as a tom-boy girl or effeminate boy).* [Emphasis ours.]

Dr. Szasz concludes this litany by saying,

Clearly, there is no childhood behavior that a psychiatrist could not place in one of these categories. To classify as pathological academic performance that is "underachievement" or "overachievement" or "erratic performance" would be humorous were it not tragic. When we are told that if a psychiatric patient is early for his appointment he is anxious, if late he is hostile, and if on time, compulsive—we laugh, because it is supposed to be a joke. But here we are told the same thing in all seriousness.[3]

Szasz believes that schools are a terrible place to have psychological services—simply because the services cannot help but be coercive. Requiring children to go through diagnosis and treatment for alleged psychological disease in school is akin to a legal commitment hearing in which a person is forced against his will into a mental institution—except that the kids have fewer rights. No matter how much school authorities insist the treatment proposed is for the child's own good, Szasz points out that the institution stands to benefit—and the relationship of the child and parent to the school is a cruelly unequal one.

He is savage with his colleagues: "The aims and results of several modern methods of psychodiagnosis resemble closely the ordeal by water (used in the Middle Ages to identify witches by drowning them)."[4]

He has scorn for projective tests such as the Rorschach or the thematic apperception test. He says that when a clinical psychologist administers such a test to a person referred to him by a psychiatrist, there is "the tacit expectation that the test will show some 'pathology' "—in other words, that merely because he is taking the test, the patient must have something wrong with him. It is the same assumption that guides all testing for emotional problems in the public schools or in private centers today.

"All this pseudomedical hocus-pocus and jargon serves to confirm the subject in the role of mental patient, the psychiatrist in the role of medical doctor, and the clinical psychologist in the role of paramedical technician (who 'tests' the patient's mind instead of his blood)," says Szasz.

And he concludes ominously: "In more than twenty years of psychiatric work, I have never known a clinical psychologist to report, on the basis of a projective test, that the subject is a 'normal, mentally healthy person.' While some witches may have survived dunking, no 'madman' survives psychological testing."[5]

Under present Special Education laws, parents are guaranteed equal-partner status in planning for their children's education. In some districts that is the case, and the parent can call a halt to the nonsense and tell the school to teach his kid in a normal class at a normal pace. But in too many districts this equal status is a pious hope.

Research says that though parents are present at meetings when their children's educational placements are discussed, the real decision making takes place before the meetings—in closed-door sessions between teachers, administrators, and counselors.

Educators also deliberately use a shorthand sort of jargon full of pseudoscientific terms designed to baffle parents and to reinforce their own authority status. James Ysseldyke, writing in the *Journal of Learning Disabilities*, said that even in situations where it was clear that they had not been able to participate in decisions made about their children, parents tended to feel impressed and satisfied with team meetings.[6]

Parents feel less expert today about knowing their kids than they did in an earlier generation. It takes a lot of parents—whose time is frequently divided severely in two-career families—years to realize that the experts actually know less about their children than they do. And what's the use of fighting it? The school system can exert tremendous pressures to force parents to accept a diagnosis they know is untrue—it happened to us and to hundreds of others who have contacted us over the past four years. The chilling thing is that the schools know this.

Laurence Lieberman, a Special Educator who teaches at Boston College, wrote a formula for bullying parents into accepting diagnoses against their children. It appeared in January 1983, in the *Journal of Learning Disabilities* and it shows how far schools will go to force a child (and his parents) into accepting a diagnosis they feel is wrong:

> A problem has arisen that had not been obvious or even in evidence prior to the proliferation of special education services. It has the potential to be one of the greatest sources of frustration to special educators.
>
> It is the unwillingness of some parents to allow services to be provided for their children regardless of perceived need and regardless of the availability of these services. . . .

Too many educators are too willing to take no for an answer, without exploring the possibilities inherent in more aggressive behavior. How many phone calls are made? How many school meetings are called? How many different teachers and administrators continuously present the same viewpoint (that the child needs help)? Finally, how much pressure is exerted on the parents? There have been cases where school systems have asked for a hearing because the parents are unwilling to sign an educational plan. It is obvious that *there are times when educators must assert themselves and preserve their own rights as professionals to pursue their professions.* [7] [Emphasis ours.]

In other words, Lieberman commends schools bullying parents into giving up their children, because educators have their own goals as professionals to pursue.

The idea of psychodiagnosis of mental illness in children—despite critics—is so entrenched in schools that the controversies surrounding it are not discussed—certainly not between parents and teachers. That's because the mere process of being accused of deviant behavior—the fault is on the part of the child and the parent—means that nothing they say means a thing anymore. The parent becomes a nonperson in the process.

In our case, we told the psychotesters that our son had speech problems but that he could read. Instead, they found he was hopelessly retarded—and that he could not read! When we pointed out that we had told them he could read, they said their tests showed that he had no prereading skills. What they would not say is the truth—that from the beginning, we had ceased to exist as persons who had anything worthwhile to say about anything, because our child was "different."

If this sounds like something out of Kafka, it is nonetheless true. Dr. Szasz says, "The mental patient is a living corpse, the words he utters the semantic exudates of his disease, to be examined, not heeded." [8]

The parents are on trial as much as their children in

these pseudoscientific hearings, and the sooner parents understand that, the better for their child. Special Educators already know it and they become annoyed when parents become hard to deal with because of it.

William E. Davis, a Special Educator who wrote a book for his colleagues on how to get along in today's schools, said,

> Still another reason why parents have come to distrust some professionals is that they perceive that *they* not the child have been viewed, correctly or incorrectly, as the "problem. . . ."
>
> Mr. Adams, the father of Chris, a nine-year-old diagnosed as autistic, was asked to meet with the local school agency's consultant psychiatrist in order to discuss the child's problem and impending program. Quite willingly, Mr. Adams kept his appointment and, as he expressed it, "I was really looking forward to finding out some way that I could help Chris." Mr. Adams related that the entire session focused on *him* and his *wife*—not Chris. The final recommendation of the psychiatrist was that he and his wife both should seek psychotherapy. As Mr. Adams said, "As I look back at that meeting, I left never feeling so guilty and helpless in my life—also bitter."[9]

How far the schools have come from the three *R*s! This sort of interference in the family, stressing that children are to be considered in relation to the "ecology," including their neighborhood and family, has been growing since the 1960s. Initially, experimentation was done on black families and now it has spread across the color spectrum to every class of American life. Teachers talk less of teaching Johnny where the capital of France is than of helping him achieve "self-esteem" and "self-image" and creating an environment for "ego development." Johnny still doesn't know that it's Paris.

In fact, teachers are only teachers. They are not psychologists and they are not therapists. They know very little about the things they talk so much about. They lack competence to judge a child's emotional state. Their information about family and family situations is guesswork. It is framed by stereotypes about economic classes and ethnic groups and even racial prejudice. Yet they have been taught in the colleges of education to regard all this claptrap as scientific information.

If emotional disturbance is such a vague and mysterious concept, how is it that educators can treat it in Special Education? Well, treatment is not quite what you might think it is. Children who fit into the emotionally disturbed category are packed off to Special Education centers, where they are subjected to something called "behavior modification." The main educational approach is to attack the problem of their unacceptable behavior directly—though some also get psychotherapy to find the cause of their emotional disturbance.

The contrast between the high philosophical rhetoric educators use before getting the child into Special Ed and the nuts-and-bolts approach they take after is startling. It reminds you of the promises of the car dealer before you sign on the dotted line and his approach to you when the transmission falls out.

One favorite approach to behavior modification is a system of rewards in the form of junk-food treats given out as a child does this or that correctly—rather the way one trains a dog. Some are given candies for learning to read new words, or they build up points for a trip to McDonald's for a Big Mac. One mother told us that behavior modification in Special Ed had added obesity to all her son's other problems.

But there is another side of behavior modification that is not merely trivial. You find that just about any program involving rewards and punishments can be called behavior modification in the schools. And if there are rewards, then there are also punishments.

We have heard from parents of children with Down's syndrome that the kids have spent long school days locked in dark closets. A woman whose son was diagnosed as autistic wrote that she once was a witness as Special Educators tied her screaming son into a chair and sprayed vinegar into his throat. The distraught mother was kept from interfering by assistants who soothed her with the assurance that this was for his own good.

Slapping and hitting these children, denying them ordinary contacts with their peers, locking them into year-round and sometimes twenty-four-hour programs with no hope of a respite, isolating them in various ways, insisting that their parents carry on with the same behavior modification systems at home—all these things happen in Special Education. The justification for them is supposedly scientific. It is all done for the good of the child. Of course, the educational treatments little boys underwent in Dickens were done for their own good, too. We adults seem to be most dangerous to children when we decide to do things to them for their own good.

And most dangerous of all is the teacher armed with a set of bogus scientific pronouncements, who has been taught that treating children like laboratory animals to be "conditioned" into doing what authority wants is not cruelty but therapy.

In truth, the educator quickly admits he doesn't understand what causes deviant behavior. Moreover, he doesn't care. He is just trying to get the child rounded off enough to be acceptable to society—that is, to the school. And this is done first of all by segregating him from other students, both physically in separate classrooms or schools and psychologically by fixing a label on him to make certain he will be considered different and apart from his normal peers.

Isolated with others also wearing labels, the child has little opportunity to judge what constitutes acceptable behavior. He becomes confused, bitter, angry.

Research has shown conclusively that children with behavior problems who are separated from the normal classroom have those behavior problems increase instead of decrease.[10] But that is the usual policy in most Special Education districts today.

Of all the children victimized by the rush to judgment of today's education system, the children labeled emotionally disturbed are the saddest of all. Their presumed diseases are so vague and mysterious and so compounded with social stigma that neither their parents nor they themselves are able to protest their innocence. Everything done to them is done in the name of treatment, "for their own good." The stigma on them is so heavy that even legal authorities recognize it.

The most widely used treatment for these children in Special Education—behavior modification—is even at its best so humiliating and demeaning that the child sentenced for having "low self-esteem" finds what self-esteem he has diminishing. Behavior modification offers no cure, and few educators believe that emotionally disturbed children can be cured.

Think of the term yourself—*emotionally disturbed*. It frightens you, doesn't it? Yet it can be tacked onto a child of six whose only crime is that he talks too much to his friend in the next row. Once labeled, he may wear the label all his educational life—and, frequently, beyond.

Of all the dirty little secrets in Special Education, treatment of such kids is the dirtiest.

9

Learning
Disabilities

Educators have been on an early-identification kick in the past decade. It is common wisdom in most educational circles that by finding children with problems early—and identifying these problems early—experts will help eliminate these problems when the children become school age.

Sounds good stated like that, doesn't it? But we've shown that both emotional and mental diagnoses are replete with a history of fraud and abuse and that the earlier children are tested, the less likely even an honestly administered test is to be accurate.

Note, too, that few in education think that children labeled retarded will get better. They can just be managed better, taught rough social skills, and kept out of the way of society. Nor do educators think children called emotionally disturbed can be helped. Yet they prattle on that the earlier they find problems in kids, the sooner they can correct them. They either have no understanding of what really goes on in Special Education today—or they are frauds.

But there is a third amorphous category that throws educators into ecstasy and which has puzzled even severe critics of other categories. We have all heard the term by now: *learning-disabled.* It is so commonly used that it has a nickname—LD. Everyone knows what LD means. Everyone knows an "LD kid." It is these children who can be most helped if found at an early age.

After all, isn't LD's old-fashioned counterpart the kids who used to have to spend summers in summer school, "catching up"? Is LD something like the old-time "remedial reading" programs? Perhaps, but not to someone like Boston College's Laurence Lieberman, who has deplored the mentality that says kids with learning disabilities can be brought back to the normal classroom.[1]

"No handicapped child has ever been 'fixed' in Special Education and sent back to the regular class. This message must be used with those [teachers] who have the singular referral agenda of 'take him out of my room.'. . . Where they truly exist, even mildly handicapped children may always require some specialized support. . . . The vast majority of children who do get permanently 'fixed,' probably weren't handicapped to begin with."

So what does LD mean?

It means a lot of things. It doesn't mean that a child does not learn, it means that he finds it harder to learn some things than others. If that sounds normal, you are wrong.

The terms thrown around enhance the core term of *LD.* In Chicago, it is "learning-disabled." In California, it is apt to be "minimally brain-damaged." A favorite word in New York is "dyslexic" to describe the same kid. Some states decide such children are "perceptually impaired." Other specialists favor really meaty terms like "hyperkinetic behavior disorder" or "neurological impairment."

Are you confused yet? There's more confusion to come. Because the whole category of kids labeled LD doesn't really mean very much.

James Ysseldyke and other researchers at the University of Minnesota and elsewhere have worked together on extensive studies on what gets a child slated for the LD class. They found that the criteria are as vague as the concept.

One of their studies showed that under the criteria most often used by schools to decide if a child suffers from learning disability a full 75 percent of the kids who were *not* labeled LD could be put in the LD classification.

It gets more weird. They also found that experts who studied evaluation records of children already in LD categories were just as likely—based on the records—to say the kids were not learning-disabled as to say they were. Those are kids already labeled![2]

Given this kind of confusion among the experts, it is no surprise that the general public is perplexed. Bombarded in the popular press with conflicting definitions of learning disability or dyslexia—and assured by experts like the Orton Dyslexia Society that a full 15 percent of the population is dyslexic, or by well-meaning parents' groups that a third of our children are learning-disabled—most people decide this must be a terribly technical area that they cannot hope to understand.

So who is an LD child?

He is hyperactive—though in the main, hyperactivity is defined by the tolerance of the teacher.

He has trouble with language, with converting symbols into meaning. This means he has trouble reading.

He does not follow directions well—again, defined by the teacher.

He is distractible.

Some have trouble telling right from left.

Some read letters or words backward or in the wrong order.

Some are clumsy and can't catch a ball.

Some look funny. You know. They don't look right. They wear glasses or they look gawky. Their eyes don't seem to focus on you right. They are victims of what one prominent writer on LD called "the Funny-Looking-Kid Syndrome."

Some have allergies.

Some throw tantrums.

Some are painfully shy.

Researchers agree that the diagnosis of learning disabilities is really a matter of exclusion; we note the child cannot be normal because he is behind in classwork (and educators would surely like to discover that any child who fails in any classroom is mentally abnormal, no matter that this would mean labeling the majority of our children defective). Then we give him an IQ test to see how smart he is and we decide his problem is not due to retardation. So we give him an eye test and that turns out all right, and we give him a hearing test and that's okay, and eventually, when we find nothing else wrong with him, we make him learning-disabled.

As the Association for Children with Learning Disabilities puts it, a child judged LD must have had "adequate learning opportunities." For practical purposes, it means he has been in a classroom. But the adequacy of the classroom and the teacher is never discussed. Never.

Researchers have found that the only thing all LD kids have in common is low achievement in class. The Association for Learning Disabilities has come up with a definition to make it sound as though there is some scientific base to labeling a child as learning-disabled; it is a beauty:

> Specific Learning Disabilities is a chronic condition of presumed neurological origin which selectively interferes with the development, integration, and/or demonstration of verbal and/or nonverbal abilities. Specific Learning Disabilities exists as a distinct handicapping condition in the presence of average to superior intelligence, adequate sensory motor systems, and adequate learning opportunities. The

condition varies in its manifestations and in degree of severity.

Throughout life, the condition can affect self-esteem, education, vocation, socialization, and/or daily living activities.

If you want to understand this definition, go back to the first sentence. Note the three key words: "presumed neurological origin." That means the child has a defective brain. It also means that there is no way to prove it, that he will always have it, and that in spite of all the educators promise to the contrary about getting a child back "in the mainstream," nobody expects the condition to be cured.

This chapter on what learning disability is and what it is not will be hard going because the experts who have studied the subject don't have the faintest idea of what learning disability is. There has been extensive research done on the subject so that whole forests have been felled to print the results—and it still comes down to a label put on a child because he or she is not doing well in class. The label itself is the important thing because it puts the burden of failure on the child and not on the classroom, the school system, the textbook, the course, the teacher, the principal, or whether the kid ate his Cheerios faithfully. And the label is required to give proof to the federal and state governments that the districts actually have LD kids and that they need more Special Education funding. Labeling is what a lot of Special Education is all about.

It is important to note, before we plunge into the discussion, that the learning-disabled population is overwhelmingly male. Ninety percent of the children labeled hyperactive—a subgroup in the learning-disability classification—are boys. It is a consistent finding that at least 75 percent of children in programs for reading disabilities are male.

Learning-disabilities enthusiasts have theorized that this must be because males are more susceptible to brain damage. This is nonsense. It could not explain this over-whelming and consistent sex difference. A more realistic explanation is offered by the psychologist Diane McGuin-ness, who has researched sex differences in education ex-tensively.

McGuinness notes that the psychotesters have always been careful to obscure the very real differences between the sexes that they have discovered over and over again. When Binet was developing his IQ test, boys consistently scored lower than girls. To eliminate the effect, Binet changed his scales to include more of the kinds of tasks on which boys do well.

The same thing happened when David Wechsler was developing a new test, which has since become one of the standards for testing children's intelligence in schools. On almost every subtest, girls initially scored better—for they are known to excel over males in language development. So the tests were changed to include such things as block design or speed in translating numbers into letters. The changes were made, educators say, to make sure the tests are fair. "However, if in the early tests more girls had received low scores than boys, it is likely that the test would not have been revised, as it would have confirmed what everyone believed," McGuinness says.[3]

The result, she believes, is that male/female differ-ences have been papered over by the psychotesting profes-sion, and schoolroom procedures that routinely deny boys the opportunity to master language skills at their own pace and in their own way have become standard. Thus, the organization of the American classroom ensures that a large number of boys—quite normal, as boys—will fail and be labeled learning-disabled.

When PL 94-142 was passed, there was a provision for a cap of 2 percent as the proportion of its school population a district could call learning-disabled to get federal funds. The cap had to be removed quickly.

By 1986 no state in the union could have met that

cutoff—and nearly 5 percent of our children were in learn-ing-disability programs. Teachers all over the country were pushing for more such identifications, and experts were asking where it would all stop.

It is a consistent finding that boys outnumber girls at least three to one in these programs—and viewed in this way, the definition of what is "abnormal" is clearly being stretched beyond common sense. The time has come to ask: Is there a point at which the public will become con-cerned? When educators have decided a fifth of our boys are defective? A quarter? A third?

Evidence for a "neurological" basis for LD is vague at best. Literally thousands of books have been written on the subject and no proof positive has been shown. Some of the more revered books in this field, which purport to convey "facts" on the "neurological" basis of learning disabilities, are nothing more than wishful thinking.[4]

As we've seen, with proof or without proof, treatments based on vague theories concerning the causes of educa-tional learning disabilities are used all the time. They can range from heavy and tragic use of psychoactive drugs ad-ministered to children who have no say over the matter, to the relatively harmless treatment of having kids walk on a balance beam without falling off. All these treatments are based on theories, not facts.

What is harder for parents to understand is that the reverse is also true: *Often, theories are developed to fit treatments that experts have decided seem to work on children!* In other words, if a child is given drugs and becomes passive and compliant and that is the reaction desired by the director of a Special Ed program, then, in time, theories develop over why the drug worked and what was "wrong" with the child's brain in the first place.

Education trade journals are full of debates about learning disabilities that would shock parents of children who have been routinely labeled LD. The journals show that the experts still have not reached the common ground of agreeing on what a learning disability is—and what to do about it.

These journals—read by teachers, psychologists, and administrators—are a hodge-podge of patched-together arguments and an occasional article lamenting the fact that there is not even a unified theory at work underpinning Special Education practices. Rather, Special Education is a system of imagery. The imagery—like much thinking about children among Special Educators—is mechanistic.

What does this mean? It means that because the Special Educators have absolutely no idea how the brain works, they keep inventing metaphors and similes to explain it that probably have no relationship to the truth—if the truth is ever uncovered.

One of the most pervasive bits of imagery—used time and again by educators to bamboozle confused parents—is that of the computer. Children's minds—they say—are like computers. A number of books on Special Education take this nonsense seriously enough so that they present quite detailed diagrams showing flow charts of information going into and coming out of the brain.

Children—say the image-makers in Special Ed—have minds like computers that receive input in the form of sights and sounds, process the information like a computer interpreting electrical impulses so that it is comprehended, and then put forth output in the form of speech, writing, behavior. You wonder what the image-makers would have used as a metaphor before the invention of the computer. Perhaps it would have been a washing machine—the mind of a child is like a washing machine in which dirty clothes are put in at one end, swirled around to be cleansed, and then squeezed through a wringer at the end of the cycle. (If the washing-machine image strikes you as nonsense—and it is—then don't be impressed or fooled by the computer image.)

Here is an example of the image-maker's art. It is a statement by Dr. Frank H. Mayfield, neurosurgeon and educator, who was quoted in *Schooling for the Learning Disabled: a Selective Guide to LD Programs in Elementary and Secondary Schools Throughout the United States:* "If the cortex can be accepted as the data processor of our human computer system and the temporal lobes as our data bank, then the special anatomical senses of vision, hearing, taste and smell along with the important tactile and kinesthetic sensations should be considered as the programmers. Sensory impressions that receive attention and those which are organized into a pattern of associations are transferred from the short-term memory area to the long-term temporal storage area behind the frontal lobes."⁵

Once the wonderful and mysterious and quite complex matter of how a child learns is reduced to mechanistic metaphors, it gets easier and easier for the frauds in Special Education to talk more nonsense and fool more parents into giving up their children's futures. Parents are told that there is something wrong with the "hardwiring" inside a child's brain, that "input" is flawed by "hardware" and "software" problems.

This violently antihuman nonsense does not lead toward respect for the child as a person. Dr. Mayfield, rhaposodizing over his beloved mechanistic metaphor, speaks of love as a "neurotransmitter" to be "drawn from the memory bank." The child is not human anymore. The child is not worthy of respect. The child does not develop himself to his best ability. He is a defective object to be tinkered with by a pro, to be dosed with chemicals.

Increasing numbers of children are put on strong psychoactive drugs when they do not act like the good computers act. One of them is the heavily advertised (in education literature) Ritalin, whose manufacturer is the CIBA drug company. It is interesting to note that CIBA first gave widespread public airing to the meaningless phrase *"minimal brain dysfunction."*

Children, in short, do not have free will, are not human beings as you and I are. Take the attitude of Dr. Harold B.

Levy, a physician, who wrote: "The child with MBD [minimal brain damage] has an organic biochemical disorder and needs medication to correct this imbalance; to suggest that he can do this by will power alone would be equivalent to demanding that a diabetic child force himself to stop spilling sugar in his urine."[6]

In other words, once the experts decide that your Johnny or Jennifer has minimal brain dysfunction or minimal brain damage—and there is absolutely no way of proving there even is such a thing as minimal brain damage—then the next logical step is to put the kid on drugs.

In fact, the evidence for this mysterious thing called "chemical dysfunction" is not evidence at all! The "evidence" consists of observations by teachers and doctors that some supposed symptoms of learning disabilities can be reduced by the use of drugs; kids become more docile and thus are thought to focus better on academic tasks.[7]

In fact, studies on learning indicate the drugs do *nothing* to help academic problems—while at the same time, the long-term side effects on children of use of these drugs, often for years, is not understood at all. It is known and accepted that children dosed with such behavior-controlling drugs experience weight loss and chronic insomnia and interruptions in their growth rate, and some of them become anxious and depressed.

Even some of the drug enthusiasts among educators say drug treatments should not be extended over more than two years—but we have received testimony from parents that their children have been maintained on Ritalin for as long as *nine years*. Some parents are assured that their children's brains are so dysfunctional that they will have to take drugs all their lives.

How many kids in Special Education are drugged? There are no hard figures. Diane McGuinness calls 600,000 to 700,000—a commonly accepted figure—a conservative estimate.[8] Several Special Education textbooks we reviewed estimated that about half the children called learning-disabled are given drugs.

Why put kids on drugs? The Special Educators say that without drugs some kids are unmanageable. The experts note that some kids even learn to ask for their pills to control themselves—having absorbed the idea that they are not personally able to take responsibility for their emotions or their performance in class. This dependent group of drug-addicted children—and if you need drugs to function or think you need them to function, you are an addict—is growing with the growth of casual diagnoses of learning disabilities.

Wait a minute, say the educators. Drugs wouldn't be used so extensively if they didn't work. Perhaps the population truly has become abnormal and drugs are needed to correct a widespread chemical imbalance in children. Prove it, we say—and there is no proof.

Writing together on the subject of drug use on school-children, a geneticist, a neurobiologist, and a psychologist concluded that it represented a shocking misuse of science. They wrote:

> [I]t is not without interest in the context of the supposed therapeutic use of Ritalin for MBD that it has been shown that whereas, on average, lower dosages may increase a child's attentiveness and "set" for learning, higher doses simply result in sedation—yet in school use it is the higher doses that tend to be employed. This makes the drug yet one more version of the chemical straitjacket, ensuring that the teacher has an easier task in maintaining classroom order, but only by doping out the children who would otherwise make it harder.

They concluded that the real effects of these drugs on children are incalculable. The idea that they are a "magic bullet" that works directly and neatly on a supposed "disease site" in the brain is foolish. "Most of the interactions of extraneous drugs with the body's chemistry are more like an explosion with shrapnel flying in many directions and a large area of fallout rather than bullets producing a neat contained hole."[9]

Yet drug use for children is often the first recommendation by doctors examining children suspected of having learning disabilities. One psychology professor wrote—after a review of studies done on drugging hyperactive children—that "recent data have shown that the proportion of drug 'responders' in a group of normal children is identical to that of a hyperactive group."[10]

In layman's language, that means that if you take a group of hyperactive kids and give some of them drugs and take a group of normal kids and give some of them drugs, the children in the two groups will respond to the drugs in exactly the same way. So who is to say who is "normal" and who is "hyperactive"?

Here is another argument the Special Educators use: Some children with identified brain lesions are often distractible and hyperactive. Therefore, if we find children who are distractible and hyperactive but we cannot find any brain damage, then the brain damage must be so small that we call it minimal brain damage.

If you like that argument—and lots of people do—then extend the argument to measles. Children with measles often act cranky and tired. If you have a child who is cranky and tired, he should be treated as though he has measles —even though we cannot find any evidence of measles in him yet!

Typical of this kind of backward logic is the activity being pursued at Boston Children's Hospital, a center for learning-disability research and a shrine to mystification of the process. The hospital is home to Dr. Melvin Levine, one of the prominent image-makers in the field, who has his own metaphor to offer a confused public: Children with learning disabilities have minds like television sets without the channel selector.[11]

The New York Times reported on work at the hospital and said: "The emerging view is that hundreds of different agents—genetic factors, drugs, hormones, infection, injury and so forth—can cause changes in brain structure or function that can lead to learning disabilities. Thus the main research strategy today is to identify anatomical, electrical and chemical differences in the brains of those afflicted and try, for the first time, to separate the disorders into biological subgroups."[12]

What lies behind that tangle of words is the idea—the unproven, base idea of Special Education and the system—that children who don't respond the way authorities want them to respond are sick.

When a child has trouble learning his multiplication tables—and perfectly reasonable, ordinary kids do have such troubles—we teach the "normal" child a new way to learn. But once we have tagged a kid as learning-disabled and *he* has trouble learning his multiplication tables, we don't try to teach him in a new way—we give him "treatments" that might consist of drugs, psychotherapy, behavior modification, or confinement to a box that is supposed to screen out distractions (a particularly frightening device used in some Special Ed classrooms), exercises to improve his "sensory integration," or—in some sad cases where hyperactivity has been diagnosed—major brain surgery.

None of these measures teach the child his multiplication tables. But that is not their intent. Their intent is to "improve the patient," to make the child more acceptable to the people who don't like him. And we don't like people or kids who are "different," do we? But, in a humane age, we want to help them, don't we?

The Orton Dyslexia Society, named for one of the pioneers in the study of dyslexia, actively solicits diagnosed dyslexics to give their brains to science after death for dissection, so that their anatomical peculiarities can be mapped. The fact that the idea of dyslexia itself is open to question does not stop the march of science. It stretches like a golden chain from the study of the size and shape of skulls in the nineteenth century right to modern-day voodoo doctors who predict future behavior by studying handwriting or practice "cranial bone manipulation" to increase learning capacity.

Why on earth do we want to compare the brains of

children to computers? If anything, computer develop-
ments have demonstrated that artifical intelligence is far
different in origin, source, and achievement from human
intelligence. Yet the image is there to seduce the unsophis-
ticated. Educators love simplicity and want parents to love
it as well. See your child as a machine and you will not have
guilt feelings in considering his wants, his feelings, his developing character. A child ceases to be an individual, his
opinions fail to count. He is a mass of inputs, outputs, and
processing deficits; he is a thing.

The Special Education researcher James Ysseldyke has
discovered that the kind of behavior that will get a child
sent to Special Education evaluation very often depends on
the teacher. In other words, a teacher decides she doesn't
like what Johnny or Jennifer does in one class and sends
him or her to Special Ed; while the same behavior in another class—with another teacher—is acceptable.

Some teachers don't like some children. It's been that
way from the beginning of education. Only recently have
teachers developed the golden cop-out: There is no need
to expel a child—just send him away to Special Education
and forget about him.

Special Educators are well aware that schools create
learning-disabled children by their rigidity and their refusal
to allow for individual differences. When the *Journal of
Learning Disabilities* published a survey of experts on the
question of how many learning-disabled children there really are, they received some intriguing answers. Several of
the educators responded that the incidence depended on
the money available to treat them. And Gerald Getman, an
optometrist who works with Special Educators, put the incidence at $33\frac{1}{3}$ percent: the number of our children who can
be demonstrated to be having problems in school. "Most
of these should not be having academic problems, and I do
not think they would be if the curriculum was designed for
them instead of expecting them to fit into a rigidly stand-

ardized, production-line program so common to most schools," he said.[13]

The statistics show that the phenomenal growth in the proportion of our children labeled learning-disabled is probably far from over. A national survey of teachers in 1981 showed that they thought 57.7 percent of their students needed special help of one kind or another; the regular curriculum was meeting the needs of only around 40.3 percent of their students. And they thought a full 10.4 percent of their classes ought to be declared learning-disabled—and another 3 percent emotionally disturbed. All together they saw a need to put a full 23 percent of their students in the handicapped categories—almost double the number we have now.[14]

If the past trends are any indication, they may well get their wish. Some already have: An Illinois Board of Education pamphlet noted in 1984 that some districts have declared 20 percent of their students eligible for learning-disability programs.[15] But as more and more defective children are labeled and segregated, it seems that more and more appear.

When similar surveys were done in the years 1966–70, before the big push to identify learning-disabled children began, teachers would have put 12 percent of their students in the handicapped categories.[16]

By 1986 we had reached that level. Will we reach the new level of 23 percent in another decade?

The whole thing is gussied up with pseudoscientific jargon, of course. The child as machine has "processing dysfunctions" and shows "indications of organic involvement." There are no bad teachers, naturally—everyone is a "concerned professional."

Making children into machines takes the heat off teachers and, too frequently, off parents who don't want to be bothered doing what is best for Johnny or Jennifer. We live in the age of the two-income household, the atomic family exploded into alienation; the last thing some parents want is to spend all that time fighting a system that promises to have all the answers when it turns out that Johnny can't read. The sad fact is that Johnny eventually grows up in that system, learns to be a failure, resents his parents—and graduates into a world in which he still can't read or write or figure.

It doesn't matter. A child is a computer. And love is only a technique of management, knowledge is only input, teachers are merely technicians minding the machines. If we continue to believe this nonsense and build a system on it, then we have lost our humanity, we have denigrated the art of teaching to the trade of fixing computers, and we have abandoned our children to a future as bleak and certain as the future shown by Scrooge's Christmas spirit.

10

Not Special
and Not Education

Up to now, we have peeled back some of the layers of gobbledygook surrounding the labeling of children in Special Education. It was important to take the time to examine labels, because a lot of Special Education is tied up in the business of putting labels on kids and making sure they stick.

All right, some educators say, so the process of labeling needs to be examined and changed. Still, if a child has some learning problems, he will get good attention to them once he is in Special Education classes—no matter what label he carries.

This seemingly enlightened point of view is shared by many educators who abhor the labeling process but think that Special Education is still doing a lot of good for a lot of kids. The argument is beguiling: If kids in Special Ed did better than similiar children left to rot in regular education, then all the faults, the enormous expense, and the vagueness of the diagnostic process in Special Education could be forgiven.

So let's ask the million-dollar question: *Does Special Education help children?* A tiny percentage. The rest are harmed—or they do no better than they would have in regular education. That's the answer. That's what dozens of comparison studies have shown.

The outstanding, unequivocal result is that educators have been unable to show that Special Education programs —*particularly* full-time segregated programs—produce better results than leaving the kids called mildly handicapped in regular classrooms.

Who does Special Education help? Generally, children with severe physical problems such as spina bifida. Parents of such tragically physically handicapped kids are often deeply grateful for state-funded Special Ed programs, and without this kind of support, these children would probably receive no education at all. We have been contacted by parents of such children who are terrified that any criticism of Special Education might dry up funding to the extent that their children would be denied an education. And Special Educators are quick to whip up panic among such parents whenever some Special Ed program or practice comes under criticism.

If a deaf child or a child in a wheelchair can benefit from a small specialized class, does that automatically mean that a child with a low IQ score or a child who has trouble remembering his short vowel sounds should be treated the same way? In other words, if Johnny has trouble reading, is he helped by being placed in a program originally conceived as a way to help severely retarded children or blind children?

We cite one study below that shows clearly that among these so-called mildly handicapped kids—the ones who have trouble with reading and writing and behaving in class

—children left in regular classrooms do better than similar children placed in Special Ed! The result is startling and is not comforting the layers of bureaucrats who have formed ranks around Special Education in the past decade.

There is money to be made in Special Ed; it is a growth industry and it spends money like a sailor on shore leave. Segregated Special Education classes routinely spend two to five times as much money on a child's education as regular classes do. Yet there is something so fundamentally wrong with this concept of segregation that studies show it still negates any good effect that Special Education might be thought to have on a child.

In 1982, the Center for Social Organization of Schools at The Johns Hopkins University in Baltimore reviewed research done on the effects of placing mildly handicapped children in full-time or part-time Special Education compared with full-time regular classes. Here is the report:

> Methodologically adequate studies of placements of academically handicapped students indicate no consistent benefits of full-time special education on any important outcomes; the research tends to favor full- or part-time regular class placement over full-time special education for the achievement, self-esteem, behavior and emotional adjustment of academically handicapped students. Differences between full-time regular class placement and part-time regular class placement with resource help tend to favor well-constructed part-time programs for achievement, but not for social-emotional outcomes.[1]

The study by the center seemed to startle the researchers as much as anyone. One of the results uncovered was that the "ideal" Special Education class program was no better than the regular class placement. This was the result, despite the fact that Special Education classes are smaller, get more funding, Special Ed teachers have special training, and the children get special treatment.

In the words of one observer, the outstanding fact

about Special Education is that it is neither very special, nor is it education.

The writers of the Johns Hopkins report were troubled: "It would seem logical that if students have serious learning problems, a setting in which specially trained teachers provide individually tailored instruction to very small classes would be ideal for remediating these problems. How could virtually pre-ordained failure relative to classmates in regular classes be more beneficial to academically handicapped students than step-by-step success in a special education class?"[2]

The question was troublesome but the researchers admitted finally that their results showed the failure of Special Education: "There is no evidence of any kind that self-contained special education is superior to placement in regular classes in terms of increasing the academic performance of mildly academically handicapped students, and the best evidence is that in general, it is regular class placement with appropriate supports that is better for the achievement of these students."[3]

This study went on to conclude that the effect of labeling children and segregating them in dummy classes was itself damaging to children—so damaging that Special Education had a high hurdle to overcome at the outset, and few kids succeeded in overcoming the hurdle.

Parents will find in their encounters with Special Educators that they do not like to talk about statistics. They do not like to talk about percentages of success, of failures, of how many kids in Special Education programs ever get out of Special Education programs. In our case, we found that the director of our local Special Education unit refused to talk about the statistics we uncovered that indicated his agency was overplacing black children in classes for the retarded—this despite the fact that such figures are matters of public record!

"I'm not going to talk numbers with you," he said brusquely. "You might be talking apples and oranges."

This intense shyness concerning statistics pervades Special Education districts throughout the country. Yet the Special Educator is quite willing to decide a child is defective because he has a larger head than some percentage of children on some table or because he fails to meet "age norms" on his drawing test or because his drawings include some number of "indicators" of emotional disturbance or because his visual-motor coordination is below the twenty-fifth percentile.

Parents should try to get specifics out of Special Educators before committing their children to the process. Talk to them about how many children—actual body-count children—are helped in their programs and returned to regular classes once the problem is solved. Ask them how many kids as a percentage of all children in the district are in Special Education—and why?

Special Educators do not want to be pinned down to the uncomfortable truth.

The truth is that the number of kids in Special Education varies wildly from district to district, without any reason at all.

The truth is that most children dumped into Special Education—particularly full-time Special Education—are not helped any more than if they had been left in regular full-time classes and treated like ordinary kids.

The truth is that there is a lot of money to be made by labeling kids and putting them in Special Education—there are new schools to build, new classrooms to construct, lucrative Special Ed bus contracts to be let, more Special Ed–trained teachers to be hired—and the accountability is minimal at best.

Honest educators will confess that there is very little difference in the kind of Special Education given to kids labeled retarded, emotionally disturbed, learning-disabled, or minimally brain-damaged. In spite of the heavy rhetoric about precisely identifying each child's weaknesses and applying sophisticated technology to remedy them, the truth is that Special Education classrooms are all pretty much the same. Visit them. See the kids, talk to the teachers, try to find out what is so special about Special Education. Special Education too often is a watered-down version of the regular school curriculum. The only thing special about it is that the kids in the special schools have been segregated from their peers and labeled dummies.

As Daniel P. Hallahan and James M. Kauffman write in *Exceptional Children: Introduction to Special Education*:

> Anyone who happens to look in on each of three special classes or resource rooms for mildly disturbed, mildly retarded, or learning-disabled children is not likely to see very different teaching techniques being used. This is not because the observer might be new to the field of special education and does not know what to look for, nor is it because the three teachers are not creative. Although advertising for educational materials would have us believe otherwise, the appropriate teaching strategies and the materials used are very nearly the same for each of the three areas.[4]

Or listen to James Ysseldyke and his colleagues who have been studying special education for years. They find that teaching of children labeled mildly handicapped differs very little from that given in the regular classroom. With learning-disabled students, they found, "teachers use the same instructional approaches, materials and techniques with LD students that they do with any other students. We could not find evidence that interventions for LD students are different than those used with others or that instruction for LD students is somehow unique."[5] Yet the machine of Special Education runs on, grinding up young lives and building a colossal edifice at great expense that comes to mean very little.

The key to Special Education today in the United States is the labeling process. Without it, Special Education falls apart. We have received hundreds of letters from parents detailing their struggle to get their children out of

Special Education, to wipe away the labels pinned on their kids by indifferent teachers, testers, and psychologists.

"If I had it to do over again, I would simply keep my son home," wrote a woman in New Mexico. "I could have taught him much more than he ever learned in Special Education. I know the argument that children need friends. Well, what they need more is to believe in themselves."

Teachers protest that mildly handicapped kids will be ostracized by their peers in regular classes and that they need a nonthreatening and nondemanding evironment. What teachers don't admit is that a teacher has the say of whether a kid is treated well in class. Some teachers routinely use Special Education to dump those kids they don't want in class. Other teachers make it hard on the slow learner by ridiculing him or her in front of classmates—there isn't a parent alive who can't remember one teacher or another making a child appear ridiculous or the butt of professorial humor.

The virulence of teachers against children who do not conform—not the occasional cruelties of other children—is the dragon of the regular classroom . . . and a teacher is the only one who can slay it.

Take our son. At a time when educators and psychologists declared he was severely disturbed, profoundly retarded, lacking in speech and hearing skills, the kid was a social success in class. Children from the school called him on the phone at night. He made friends in every environment—particularly the YMCA and in the neighborhood where we lived. When he had difficulties in class, other kids helped him.

Children learn cruelty from the attitudes of adults. The chief adult in the classroom should be the teacher—but too many teachers run their classes on automatic pilot, in a variation of the prison "barn-boss" system.

Teachers know the truth of what we have just said. Too many in the teaching ranks exploit labels pinned on kids. One mother told us of pressure she was under from teachers to accept an emotionally disturbed label for her son.

"If there was a playground incident, it was my son's fault," she recalled. "If he hit someone, it was because he was aggressive and disturbed. He was hit, it was because normal children won't tolerate a disturbed child." The woman continued to resist labeling her son, and after a year the teachers gave up, and that's when the reports of his "abnormality" stopped.

At this point, some educators would protest that they make efforts to include Special Education kids in regular classes as much as possible. It's called *mainstreaming* and it is a very trendy word in Special Education. Mainstreaming, in fact, is required by law—under PL 94-142 children are supposed to be put in "the least restrictive environment" possible so that they can associate with their peers as much as possible—but it's a law without teeth.

Disposition of any given child is up to the experts. If the experts agree that he doesn't belong in a regular class, he won't go to a regular class. The statistics say that the pretense that large numbers of children are mainstreamed is a sham.

Even though federal statistics have shown that the number of children with genuinely handicapping medical conditions is going down every year, the proportion of children in segregated classes has stayed the same or increased slightly over the last decade. Now, however, more of these classes are occupied by learning-disabled or emotionally disturbed or educable mentally handicapped children instead of deaf or blind or orthopedically impaired children.

"The so-called 'mainstreaming' controversy appears to be largely academic in most States," according to a report on handicapped children prepared for the U.S. Department of Education.

Child count data compiled by the U.S. Office of Special Education and Rehabilitative Services indicate that there has been little overall change in the kinds of environments in which handicapped children are taught. . . . With the exception of the speech impaired . . . none of the groups has exhibited change in the direction of a greater proportion of pupils receiving instruction in regular classes. Indeed, for the mentally retarded—the group that has received the most attention in connection with the controversy over "mainstreaming"—the bulk of the change has been in the opposite direction.[6]

Every year the number of mildly handicapped children assigned to full-time segregated Special Education classes goes up. These children are the losers, being taught to be losers—and everyone knows it.

Harry N. Chandler, associate editor of the *Journal of Learning Disabilities*, wrote in 1982 that a survey of Special Education teachers he made showed that most expect the children they believe to have "neurological problems" to remain in Special Education classes all their school lives.

" 'When we send even our best LD kids back to the regular class, they just sit there and wait to be taught,' one harassed teacher told me," Chandler writes. " 'We think that we have them ready to be mainstreamed, but we can't teach them to think. Kids in regular classes just have to do too much for themselves.' "[7]

Parents of children in Special Education classes have noticed that their kids become more and more passive and dependent the longer they are in Special Education. And research shows that what happens in Special Education classes is appalling: *Despite the smaller size of such classes, the actual time each student spends on academic tasks is not greater than the time regular students spend on such tasks—about forty-five minutes a day.*[8]

According to Ysseldyke, one important thing that distinguishes Special Ed classes from regular classes is that kids in Special Ed get a lot more praise and positive response when they perform well. This is supposed to build up their self-esteem. In fact, it does not. In fact, it has the opposite effect. Research shows that children appear to know very well that the praise they are getting in Special Ed classes is undeserved and is showered on them only because they have already been judged inadquate to participate in education with "normal" children. Children in Special Education classes frequently come to distrust the adults they work with and to believe they have no respect for them. Children know when they are being conned, and a lot of Special Education is a giant con game, worked on both parents and children.

Is anything special about Special Education except the name? Smaller class sizes is always cited. The classes are, in fact, usually smaller. But the truth is that a small classroom that contains only problem children can be an extremely stressful place. Even Special Educators talk about teacher burnout from dealing with nothing but problem children. Faced with a class full of rejects from the rest of the school, such teachers quickly become disillusioned and harassed. And this can affect the children in such classes even more.

David Melton, in his book *When Children Need Help*, tells of his own son's experiences in a special class: "If there are only eight of these children in a classroom, it would seem that they receive more individualized attention. But the question is attention to which need. Each one of these children had not just one problem; each had numerous problems. It was obvious that each one of the children offered ten times the problems that 'average' children present a teacher. This wasn't a classroom of just eight children; it was equivalent to handling a class of eighty children."[9]

Melton came to believe that placing a perfectly average child in such a class could cause him to act retarded, braindamaged, or emotionally disturbed over the course of time. He concluded that if he had it to do over again, he would teach his child at home rather than allow him to go into a special class.[10]

Separate Special Education classes do not work for the children in them. The children in Special Education do not improve their academic performance as compared to similar children in regular settings. And the effect of being labeled and segregated in Special Education can leave a scar on a child that he carries all his life.

Then why does Special Education expand so? Could it be, as many critics have written, that educators need the labeling and the pseudoscientific mystification to enhance their prestige and justify their failures?

An associate professor of education at California State University noted the growth and wrote that eligibility criteria for learning-disabled students are set so that such classes can be filled. "If funds are available, classes will appear," wrote Harold M. Murai, Ph. D. "Most teachers in the regular classrooms are delighted to be relieved of some of their students for part if not all of the school day." More money means more disabled students, Murai and others in the field believe.[11]

And clinical consultant Gerald Coles writes: "It is my firm impression that educators, *consciously* or not . . . have sought affiliation with the medical world not only because multi-disciplinary work is valued but also because it provides them with an aura of greater knowledge, authority, and importance. And who can blame them? How mundane to tell someone you teach remedial reading. How awesome to announce that you do clinical work with minimally brain-dysfunctional children, more dyslexic than dyscalculic, who are benefitting from methylphenidate."[12]

Where are the children in this? Where is real teaching? And what are educators doing but engaging in outright fraud when they tell parents Special Education exists only to help their child?

Michael Scriven delivered a paper on the subject at a Wingspread Conference on Special Education held in 1981 in Wisconsin. He said: "Special education placement showed no tangible benefits whatsoever for the pupils. Either someone thinks otherwise or else the placements continue to be made for reasons other than benefits to pupils."[13]

That is our conclusion as well. In the next chapter, we are going to help parents deal with the terminology of Special Education and to arm themselves with knowledge of what it really means when teachers throw out diagnoses and labels and theories.

11

Breaking Through the Special Ed Jargon Jungle

Consider this chapter a cram course in the pseudoscientific language used by professionals in Special Education.

Parents are rendered helpless by Special Educators, psychologists, and administrators who retreat into the jargon jungle whenever they are asked a specific question about Johnny or Jennifer and what Special Education is going to do for them.

Remember that professional educators and psychologists speak a coded language, just as other professional groups do. The average parent is not required to master all the jargon used in the auto-repair trade or the computer-programming profession or the air-traffic-controllers' job. He is required, however, to learn what the educators are talking about when they are talking about kids.

Learning what the jargon means can often clear up

mysterious diagnoses of a child's Special Education problems. Being armed with a knowledge of what the words mean—and what they don't mean—can often save parents years of frustration and misery in dealing with the strange and growing world of Special Education. Keep in mind that when you catch an educator using a meaningless term, he or she will often shift ground. Usually they will say that even if their diagnosis of minimal brain dysfunction or whatever is without meaning, the child is still in need of special help.

This sounds persuasive. But remember that children are not supposed to be labeled handicapped just because their schoolwork or school behavior does not please someone. If educators press you to sign a paper agreeing your child is handicapped in order to get him an education—when you don't believe he is—there is something seriously wrong with your school.

These questions are a compilation of the questions we have received over the years from concerned and confused parents. The answers are really plain-language summaries of all the points raised in this section.

Q. A woman who helps families deal with schools on Special Education–placement issues tells us that our son cannot be put in a class for the retarded without his adaptive behavior being studied. What is adaptive behavior?

A. Experts use adaptive-behavior scales allegedly to counteract the problems inherent in judging children solely on the basis of IQ scores (which, as we have shown, are mostly malarkey anyway).

Adaptive behavior is a way of looking at a child who tests poorly in school to see how he operates outside of school.

For example, Johnny may test low on the IQ test, but outside of school he is an active, growing, healthy boy who rides a bike, plays on a football team, shops at the grocery for his mother, is able to beat the family at video games, mixes well with his age group, and is okay in every way. Adaptive-behavior scales are supposed to make sure that the total child is taken into account when considering whether he should be placed in a class for retarded kids.

Unfortunately, in practice, a real examination of adaptive behavior is time-consuming, expensive, and rather messy. It involves the kind of subjective judgments that educators cannot define as a test score. It involves talking to parents about what is right with the child, while most parents will find that Special Educators would much rather talk about the child's "deficits." Consequently, adaptive behavior is frequently mentioned but rarely given more than lip service in Special Education evaluations.

Q. Our daughter's teacher says that she has something called "aphasia." What is aphasia?

A. In adults, it is a condition that results from having a stroke or a severe head injury. A person with aphasia has lost his ability to communicate or his speech is impaired and he has a problem in understanding and formulating language.

There is speculation—but little research work—that says similiar conditions occur in kids who have been brain-damaged at birth. If this could be demonstrated, then any child who had difficulties with language could be called brain-damaged. For a teacher to make a snap diagnosis of aphasia is ridiculous.

It is quite possible that some very bright children have trouble using and understanding language at an early age —and later grow out of it. Einstein said he did not talk fluently until he was ten, and Woodrow Wilson did not know the alphabet until he was nine. Winston Churchill, one of the greatest speakers of our time, had to develop his own training program to get himself over his difficulties with speaking.

Unfortunately, IQ tests and other psychometric examinations put heavy emphasis on judging a child's use of language as a sign of intelligence. It is critically important that parents understand this and insist that if a child is having difficulty in language some other form of test be given to him.

A sympathetic teacher can do a great deal to expand a child's use of language—just as a parent can. It is too bad that far too many public school "speech therapists" are heavily oriented toward correcting pronunciation and making sure a child's language is "appropriate" (which means simply that a child follows orders and gives expected responses to questions).

In one case a child undergoing alleged speech therapy in a public school was asked to count to 20. He did so. Then he was asked to count to 20 again. He rebelled and said, "I just did that." The speech therapist said this response was "an inappropriate use of language" and showed the child had great difficulty with understanding directions!

Q. A psychologist evaluated our son and told us that he exhibits signs of immaturity. He says he should be in a multi-categorical class for mildly handicapped children, so that he can have time to mature. This isn't the same thing as being told he is retarded, is it?

A. It seems as though it's almost always boys who are held to be immature in the schools. They talk too much, don't pay attention, maybe their speech is less sophisticated than the girls', maybe they reach out to explore things with their hands when teachers think they should be sitting still and listening. Educators who really don't have a lot against a child—not enough to want to put him away in Special Education—often suggest holding him back in school to give him time to "mature." We think there are probably times and situations where that might be done without any great effect, but we don't think it's the overall solution to the problem of male/female differences. The psychologist Diane McGuinness has made a special study of this problem. She concludes that the theory that boys are just *slower* than girls to mature can't stand up. The truth is that they mature differently—with the most important difference being that their language skills take longer to mature and, in fact, across age groups never seem to catch up with girls'.[1]

Is the solution, then, to work out a way for schools to be more accommodating to the way boys want to learn— or simply to flunk the majority of our boys until they achieve the level of verbal and attentional "maturity" that teachers prefer? We see no reason why a supposedly immature child can't be allowed to grow up along with the others his age in a regular classroom—except classroom rigidity.

Q. My son has been diagnosed as having "attention-deficit disorder." Is this an emotional disease?

A. It's simple gobbledygook. In plain English, it means your son doesn't pay attention in class. It is not a disease. Why teachers won't use plain English in talking to parents is one of the appalling questions clouding Special Education and the whole education process.

Q. We were shocked when school authorities told us our daughter has "autistic tendencies." We are heartsick because she seems very responsive to us at home and with her friends. What should we do?

A. Don't panic. "Autistic tendencies" is an increasingly popular snap diagnosis. Take the first word. *Autistic* refers to a condition in some children that exhibits itself in many strange ways. First, it is thought to apply to kids who test in the severely retarded range. They turn away from people, they are violently resistant to change, they become involved with objects in puzzling ways, they often repeat actions obsessively, and they use language in bizarre ways —or refuse to speak at all. The condition is little understood in the medical profession.

At one time, autism was thought by some to be caused

by rejecting parents. The current fad is to think that it is caused by some organic disorder in the brain—but there are no proofs of this.

Now to your case. You see your daughter as normal and affectionate and responsive. Someone at school sees her differently. In what way is she behaving with autistic tendencies? Demand plain answers. It may mean that she is not responding to the evaluator the way he thinks she should respond. It might be as simple as your daughter not answering questions promptly or not looking a teacher in the eye. Maybe she talks to herself at times in class or indulges in what used to be called daydreaming. Perhaps she twists her hair when sitting in class or maybe she fidgets.

Are these signs of autism? Or are they signs of normality? Before you accept any judgment, have a heart-to-heart talk with both the evaluator and your daughter.

Q. Our son acts up at school. We are now told he has a behavior disorder. What does this diagnosis mean?

A. It is not a diagnosis. It is claptrap dressed up to look official and vaguely medical. It simply means your son acts up at school. It says nothing but the obvious.

What is making him act up at school? That's the harder question, and it can be ducked once a pseudo-diagnosis is made. The school will probably suggest that your son go into Special Education or, if he is in Special Ed now, that he be given behavior-management treatment—or be put on drugs.

Q. Our son has been in behavior management for two years now and we definitely see an improvement.

A. Good. Much of behavior management strikes us as common sense dressed up with pseudoscientific terminology—and some of it can be very damaging.

Of course children ought to be told the rules, and those rules ought to be emphasized by the results of good or bad work. But the trouble with behavior management, a term that has come to mean just about any system of reward and punishment, is that it can quickly degenerate into a series of Mickey Mouse bonuses for things children ought to be learning to do for their own satisfaction.

In some schools, kids are told to sit quietly and they will get a reward on Friday—maybe a treat at the nearby McDonald's. One parent of a second-grader on behavior management told us that the main reward for good behavior in his Special Education school was permission to spend Friday afternoon watching slasher movies like *Friday the 13th*!

Under such a system, the child gradually becomes more and more helpless, seeing himself not as a responsible human being with rights and responsibilities but as a hopeless dependent who needs others to organize his behavior for him. There is little chance that such a regime will ever enable the child to function as an independent learner.

Q. Our eight-year-old has been diagnosed at school as being mildly handicapped. Is this the same as being retarded?

A. It's unusual for educators to stop with this general diagnosis. All it says is that your son is having some sort of problem in a regular classroom. Mildly handicapped is an umbrella term that covers a wide range of terms—learning-disabled, educably retarded, or mildly emotionally disturbed. The sad truth is that the difference between these categories is usually irrelevant. The usually recommended treatment for all of these supposedly mildly handicapped kids is to put them in the Special Education bin and give them a watered-down, undemanding version of the regular curriculum and—if there is a counselor around—give them counseling.

It is a shame that the education establishment has used the laws meant to help all kids get schooling to develop two classes of children now called handicapped. The first class of handicapped children is genuine and has always been recognized as such—kids with physical problems, kids with medical ills like Down's syndrome or cerebral palsy, children who are blind and deaf—but it's no more than 3 or 4 percent of the school population.

To boost the figures—and enrich the growing field of Special Ed—a second class of handicapped children has been formed, and it is growing by leaps and bounds. These kids are handicapped in the eyes of the educators who dump them into Special Ed. They are called behavior-disordered or educable retarded or perceptually impaired or dyslexic. What these kids need is good teaching, patience, and love—commodities sorely missing in too many of today's classrooms. What they do not need is pseudomedical treatment for imagined ills based on phony diagnoses.

Q. My wife and I are just sick with worry these days. We want to do the right thing for our son but we don't know where to turn. He has been evaluated at the urging of the school, and the testers say he is severely learning-disabled and will have to go to a special school. We want to fight this diagnosis. We think it is wrong. But we are only parents and a psychologist friend has told us that we are simply suffering from "denial" of our son's problems and we are incapable of being objective. He said we will have to undergo a "grieving" process to overcome our denial.

A. More neo-Freudian nonsense. Anytime a parent disagrees with the judgment of a psychologist or teacher, the professionals nod sagely to each other and agree that the parent is suffering from "denial." They explain that children are ego-extensions of parents and parents are unable to admit defects in their kids.

It is rot and should be called what it is. If anything, our experience and mail responses show us that too many parents in this age of the exploding atomic family and the two-career household are willing to relinquish their children's futures to the experts' diagnostic machine.

Most parents of truly handicapped children that we have met are courageous, clear-eyed people who are very honest—to others and themselves—about the failings of their children. But they are also deeply committed to finding the good in their children and building on their strengths.

Education "experts" say parents cannot be objective about children—while they can be. We want to know *why* anyone has to be objective about kids. Children are not objects. They are not TV sets, they are not computers, they are not washing machines—they are human beings. Despite the pseudoscientific base for educational testing, no one yet has been able to reduce the mystery of humanity to a measurable standardized test. If anyone tells you they have, he is lying.

Parents know more about their child than any expert could possibly learn in a few hours of tests. If you disagree with the expert—even if he has a dozen diplomas on the wall—then go with your own instincts about your child.

Q. My daughter's first-grade teacher says she thinks my girl has dyslexia. What is dyslexia? Does this diagnosis mean she will never learn to read?

A. *Dyslexia* is a catchall word that means a child has reading problems of some sort. Originally, it was used to describe a weakness apparent in some children who have difficulty in following the left-to-right march of letters and words across a page—they might read *was* instead of *saw*, or *on* for *no*. These kids also show signs of trouble telling left from right or top from bottom.

Teachers who slowly and painstakingly take such children through phonics training—expending time and energy in having the kids trace letters and break down words into sounds—find the weakness can be overcome. Unfortunately, phonics as a method of teaching reading continues to be in disfavor in large parts of the education establishment.

In recent years, dyslexia has become a dustbin category applied to any child who doesn't catch on to reading immediately. Many teachers use it as an excuse to give up on teaching a child to read. Too many teachers talk about the difficulty of teaching some children to read and blithely explain that our society puts too much emphasis on reading as a skill—who needs to read when we can watch television? Watching television is even taught as a course in some teachers' colleges, and teachers intent on giving up the idea of teaching talk too many parents into giving their child a tape recorder and letting him develop "alternate sensory pathways" to learning. This baloney—if accepted by parents—leads to lifelong illiteracy.

We feel more nonsense has been written about dyslexia than any other topic in education. *It is true* that a very small group of children have tremendous difficulty in mastering reading—but even these rare cases can learn to read with proper, attentive, and caring instruction.

Q. My daughter's teacher agrees with you that much of the labeling of children in Special Education is questionable. But in our school, she says, they have eliminated the problems by putting mildly handicapped children in "noncategorical" programs where they can get real help without being labeled. Doesn't this sound like a good idea?

A. Noncategorical programming recognizes the fact that the children called educable retarded, mildly emotionally disturbed, or learning-disabled are all treated just about the same in Special Education. That being the case, educators ask, why not skip the evaluations and just put them all together?

The trouble with that is that the child is still treated as defective, still saddled with low expectations and theories about what his "disease" is, still segregated from "normal" children. It's just that it's all done much less formally.

Under noncategorical programming, notes Special Educator Laurence Lieberman,

> the new definition of a handicap is poor school performance —or school becomes a new handicapping condition. If the

child does not have to be declared impaired, defective, disturbed, disabled, exceptional, or handicapped in order to receive special education services, then all he needs to be is different or discrepant with regard to where his classroom teacher thinks he should be in terms of learning or performance or behavior. It is easy to understand how this could lead to over-referral and under-responsibility.[2]

Once again, we think you have to ask your child's teacher to explain precisely what your child does wrong and just why your child cannot receive the teaching attention she needs in a regular classroom.

Q. We took our child to a psychologist for testing and he said the boy showed evidence of having "echolalia." What is that?

A. Children who have difficulty following language often repeat what has been said to them rather than responding in their own words. You say: "Get the sandwiches." He says: "Get the sandwiches?" Or you may say: "What did you do at school today?" And he will say: "School today?" ¬epeating the last words of the longer sentence. This is echolalia—it is a symptom and not a disease. It is a symptom of language problems. It means the child still does not have sufficient ability to follow speech without using a technique that might be described as reaching out and touching the words to make them more familiar. In other words, he repeats words to examine them more closely, not caring that the conversation has gone on without him.

Some teachers become agitated by children who do this. Many seem convinced that this in itself is evidence of emotional disturbance or that it is done deliberately to mock the teacher.

We have found that such behavior can be worked through if those around the child are patient and want the child to succeed. Sometimes it is a passing aberration that disappears in time by itself; sometimes it is a symptom related to an undiscovered physical problem, including poor vision or hearing loss.

Q. Our daughter was tested at school and was found to be educable mentally handicapped. We are confused. Does this mean she is retarded? Is it the same thing?

A. In most states, a child who is called educable mentally handicapped (also known as educable retarded) has scored between 70 and 55 on the standard IQ test.

Note that this is a range of only 15 points. Just about anyone in the field will tell you that a few points on a test should not be overinterpreted. For instance, your daughter may have scored 68—3 more points and she would have been in a different category.

If you question the test—and you should—the school officials will doubtless tell you that the diagnosis has been made on factors other than the IQ score. *Make absolutely sure you know and understand and agree with these "other factors."*

A child judged educable mentally retarded is assumed to be learning at a slower-than-normal rate. Most experts explain to parents that this means the child will fall further and further behind other kids in his age group as the years go on. This is theory, not fact. Some in Special Education feel that these "slow learners" ought to be given special help in certain areas to bring them up to regular classroom levels—and not consigned to the Special Ed bin where they *will fall further and further behind* because of the watered-down nature of the usual Special Ed course offering.

You should be aware that few children ever shake off the retarded label pinned to them during their school careers—even in later life. Nearly 60 percent of the children in this country designated EMH—educable mentally handicapped—are in full-time segregated special classrooms or in separate programs for most of their school lives, enough to drastically separate them from their "normal" classmates.[3]

You should also become aware of the fate of EMH kids. Expectations for them are generally low. The standard textbooks in the Special Ed field tell teachers that such kids will learn to do academic work at a sixth-grade level—as a maximum. More disturbing than this is the lack of accountability in EMH programs. We have discovered high-school-age children with near-normal IQ scores who have been in EMH for years—*and are reading at a first- or second-grade level.* The emphasis in American education is to keep these children happy and docile—rather than to push them to their potentials and to overcome their learning difficulties.

Q. Our son's teacher recommends that we take him to a doctor to be examined for hyperactivity. He has certainly been a handful for us. Tell us about hyperactivity.

A. Hyperactivity has been described by one psychologist as "a diagnosis in search of a patient."[4] Some time ago, drug companies came up with compounds that could control children by making them drug-docile in the classroom. At that time, there was no such thing as hyperactivity. Now it is all the educational rage—Diane McGuinness estimates that upward of 700,000 children are regularly dosed with powerful psychoactive drugs like Ritalin to control hyperactivity.[5]

It is noteworthy that nearly 90 percent of hyperactive kids are boys. A growing body of skeptics think hyperactivity is not a disease at all but a range of behavior normal for boys.

Too many doctors are willing to prescribe drugs routinely for children described by their teachers as hyperactive. This may be what your son's teacher has in mind. Remember, however, statistical evidence points to no good effect on learning in the cases of children dosed with drugs for hyperactivity. At the same time, the drugs have awful side effects—insomnia, weight loss, depression, anxiety, psychological dependence.

Q. My son's teacher told us she thought he was retarded. We told her that he can read and that he reads well. She said that he suffers from "hyperlexia." What does that mean?

A. More mystification from the education factory. It is presumably the opposite of dyslexia and is a trendy new disease in neuropsychology. It means that a child does not please his teacher, flunks his IQ tests, and yet shows a perverse ability to read that must not have anything to do with intelligence. The cause of the disease is postulated to be some sort of minimal brain damage.

All this is simple nonsense. Children who can read and understand what they read are not retarded. Period. It sounds as though the teacher has it in for your child. Talk to her—and talk to a lawyer.

Q. The school our daughter goes to wants to test her for possible Special Education placement. I was reluctant at first, but they explained to me that our state requires the school to draw up an "individualized education program" for her and that I will be an equal partner in approving it.

A. If you believe that, we have a bridge to sell you—the one that connects Manhattan and Brooklyn.

An IEP is required for all children designated for Special Education; it's federal law. It is supposed to designate objectives for the school year and state how they will be achieved. Parents sit in as part of the committee that draws up the IEP. *But they have little or no say in its design.* Further, there is absolutely no assurance that the procedures set forth in the design are going to be followed.

By the time parents get to the IEP stage, they have already agreed that their child should be in Special Education. If they object to the IEP at this point, they will find that in most states their child's new status is "handicapped," and it would be extremely difficult to get him back into the regular program.

Q. When we agreed to place our child in a Special Education program, we were told that in our school district it is policy to place the child in the "least restrictive environment." So he was not put in a separate class but was given resource help a few hours a week. However, after a few months, he was suddenly moved to a separate classroom all the time. He hates it. Can the district do this?

A. Yes. You are supposed to have some say in it and you can appeal to an administrative hearing panel to protest it but we emphasize again and again this simple fact about Special Education: *Once a parent agrees his child is handicapped, it is pretty much up to the school experts to decide what is the least restrictive environment for the child, where he should go to school, how he should be taught and what his goals will be.* The law looks like it protects parents but it does not.

Q. Our school has mainstreaming—that's better than regular Special Education, isn't it?

A. Mainstreaming means kids already labeled handicapped are selectively reintegrated into regular classrooms, usually for part of the day.

Once kids are pulled out of "normal" classes and given their handicapped labels, they often experience great difficulty in getting back into the regular-class rhythm. One grave problem is that children in the mainstream become aware—often through teachers—that Johnny or Jennifer is "emotionally disturbed" or "retarded" or "learning-disabled." This makes it hard on the special kid, even if he is part of a mainstreaming program.

Further, too many regular teachers show little patience with students they know are labeled as mental defectives. *A sincere mainstreaming effort requires more than just dumping the supposedly handicapped child back into the regular classroom.* Frankly, teachers' groups often oppose mainstreaming and regular-education teachers, in particular, resent having to spend part of their work week on kids they regard as defective. Educators say that mainstreaming is the new wave in education but the fact is that every year, the number of "mildly handicapped" kids in segregated special classrooms goes up.

Q. Testers at our local Special Education facility say our daughter, who is twelve, has a mental age of eight. How can they determine this?

A. They can't. It's a fraud and an old one in psychology. Mental age was the invention of our old friend, Alfred Binet, the Frenchman who dreamed up the IQ test. He calculated mental age by finding out what level of difficulty of a task a child could accomplish. If a child could do what an average eight-year-old could do—and no more—then he had a mental age of eight.

It's a worthless idea on the face of it, and many psychologists have acknowledged this. Binet had to first invent the task, figure out what was normal, and then control all the variables to make certain the results were scientific and were not influenced by outside factors. Of course, he couldn't do it—but the French government used his results anyway and the IQ test has passed into history as one of the most widely believed frauds in civilized society.

Too often parents are bamboozled by educators who insist the child should be treated according to his mental age and not his chronological age—as though children were fixed stars in a painted sky, never growing or learning. Your child was given an IQ test and that's all there is to it.

Q. Tests prove our son suffers from minimal brain dysfunction. But nobody seems to know what we should do about it.

A. Nobody has ever been "proved" to suffer from minimal brain dysfunction. Minimal brain dysfunction and minimal brain damage is no brain damage at all. It does not mean it is small brain damage—it means it cannot be found. Anyone who tells you they have "proved" it exists through tests should be sued for malpractice.

The term was selected by a study group in the old Department of Health, Education and Welfare—God knows why—from among thirty-eight terms used to describe children that teachers thought were odd. This happened in 1966. This same learned group also identified ninety-nine symptoms that characterize MBD syndrome. The list goes on and on, ranging from hyperactivity to "equivocal neurological signs." Under the criteria used in schools, just about any child can be said to suffer from minimal brain dysfunction. *However, the diagnosis only appears when a teacher doesn't like something about a child's classroom behavior and needs an excuse to get rid of him.*

Logically, since the disease does not exist, there is no cure for it, either. The only way kids can overcome school problems is by getting good, firm, loving instruction from a sympathetic adult. We suggest you concentrate on that goal, rather than worrying about your son's supposed brain defects.

Q. I am furious. My son spent two years in a class for educable mentally retarded children until we got him retested on the IQ test. The retesting shows he is normal and that he has wasted two years in the wrong classroom. How could a school make such a mistake? Isn't misdiagnosis illegal?

A. The law says it is illegal. But the law is toothless. Generally, as long as a school district shows it followed proper procedures—including the proper papers in a child's file with your signature to agree to testing—the chances of losing funding or being investigated are nil. *Parents have to take greater responsibility when dealing with their child's education.* It is too important to leave in the hands of the educators anymore.

Q. Our grandson's trouble in school is caused by "mixed dominance." What does that mean?

A. Mixed dominance or mixed laterality means a person shows an inconsistent preference in using the right and left sides of his body—he may write with his left hand and throw with his right, he may be left-eyed and right-handed.

Most kids develop a decided hand preference by age five. Those who don't sometimes have problems—especially if the problem is connected with a difficulty in using both eyes together properly. A number of researchers have found a relationship between mixed dominance and reading problems. Unfortunately, the research is inconclusive and includes speculation that mixed dominance is caused by some sort of brain damage.

Forget the speculation and theory. It is known that children with this problem can benefit from exercises and drills aimed at increasing their awareness of left and right, as well as realizing their own position in space. Interesting work is being done in this area by developmental optometrists, and they might be able to help your grandson. Look at chapter 16, where we explore the problem of vision and what can be done to improve it.

Q. The Special Education teacher my daughter has is enthusiastic about a new program she calls "modality training." What is it?

A. Modality training was very popular in education circles a few years ago. The idea is that all children can be separated into either auditory learners or visual learners. You find out whether a kid learns better through his eyes or ears, and then beam your learning message at the "preferred modality."

After a lot of work and experimentation, studies show that modality training doesn't work. Some educators, however, haven't gotten the message yet. We think the reason teachers still talk about this is that they like the word *modality;* it sounds scientific.

Q. At a preschool screening, the examiner discovered my daughter was "perseverating" and was very concerned about it. What does that mean?

A. All it means is that she continues with a response after it is no longer appropriate. It means a child can't change the subject of his or her thoughts as quickly as we would like. Too many quickshooters think it indicates emotional disturbance or retardation.

Unfortunately, there is no way of knowing if your examiner really understands the term. Too many of them confuse perseveration with repetition, and they are not the same thing. Children—especially preschoolers—often repeat words as a way of helping them understand the words better, and for the same reason they can be slow in following shifts in conversation. Yes, you should be concerned about anything that may cause your child trouble in school, but this may not necessarily be a serious matter. Work with your daughter on language development. Remember that a parent is a child's primary teacher.

Q. Our child has trouble learning to read. The evaluator at the local Special Education district told us he has "soft neurological signs indicating brain damage." We are just heartbroken and want to know what we have to do for him.

A. When a psychologist says a child has soft neurological signs, he means the child does not have any real signs of brain dysfunction. The psychologist is saying your child acts odd and maybe there is something wrong with his brain—even though there is no evidence of brain damage.

Does that make sense to you? Not to us either. Soft neurological signs can range from talking too much to poor reflexes, depending on which psychotester you're talking to.

Ignore the phrase and concentrate on working on your son's reading problem. Chances are some careful and patient work on phonics will help him a lot.

Q. My daughter's teacher wants to put her in Special Education because she needs a "multisensory approach" to learning. What do you think?

A. A multisensory approach means the child not only reads a word but uses other senses to emphasize it in memory:

She says it aloud, she traces the letters with her finger, et cetera. A lot of the success of the Montessori schools, for example, appears to be in affording children these sorts of experiences. The question we have is simple: If this method of teaching is so good for so many kids—and it is—why is it confined to Special Education? Isn't it just good old-fashioned commonsense teaching? Why do kids have to be labeled retarded or brain-damaged before they are taught?

All the questions of all the parents who want to know about Special Education are not answered in this chapter—though if you read the whole book, there are a lot more answers buried in these pages. In addition, we have included a very selective bibliography of other good books on the subject and books that will help parents help their kids overcome school-based problems.

The important thing for parents is to realize they have the right to demand that anyone making a judgment on their child *tell them in plain English what the judgment means.* Phonies hide behind jargon. Unfortunately, you may meet a lot of phonies in the Special Education jungle.

PART THREE

The New Segregation

12

You Are Not Alone

We told our story in the first place in order to speak out and show other parents that they are not alone in questioning some of the testing and procedures of Special Education.

When we first wrote about this in the pages of the *Chicago Tribune* over three years ago, we—and the *Tribune* editors—were stunned by the response. It was immediate and it has never stopped. Hundreds and hundreds of letters—and then thousands—poured into *Tribune* offices and nearly all of them were positive, and thousands of them told of other parents fighting other fights in the Special Education war.

Later, we wrote our story for *Reader's Digest,* and again the response was incredible—this time from every state in the Union. We not only got stories from parents but from teachers, principals, school administrators, Special Education therapists, optometrists, and even a few brave psychologists who agreed that too much nonsense was being peddled these days about kids and how we label them and how we fail to teach them.

We realized that the single biggest problem facing parents who are going to have to fight for their child's right to a free and normal education was the sense that the parent stood alone against a vast system. It is easier to fight city hall these days than the local school district. *But it is also possible to fight and to win on behalf of your child!*

How you fight and how you win is part of the message of the last section of this book. In this and the following chapter, we are going to share with parents information gleaned from all the people who have talked to us, written to us, or called us over the years to tell their own Special Education stories.

All of the letters and conversations depicted below are real and they all come from people who were willing to give us their names and addresses. However, although we are listing the towns where these people live—and their initials—we are going to give them privacy so that they will not be harassed physically or verbally as we were when we told our story.

Listen to the voices.

J.H. OF NORTH BALTIMORE, OHIO: I just want to say that you deserve a medal for not letting your son in Special Education classes. I taught in Special Education both as a teacher for learning disabilities and slow learners and I saw the problems the parents face. The labeling may not always start with the psychologists. Just sit in a teacher's lounge and listen to the conversation sometime. I had to test each student in my class at the end of the school year and write up an IEP [individualized education program] for each student. I had to be very careful to show only a slight improvement in order to keep the federal funding for the program and the same number of students in the class. Students in

Special Education classes are made to feel inferior not only by their classmates but by the regular teachers. Parents must be willing to buck the system and not listen to the so-called experts when they know they are right.

A.W. OF GROVES, TEXAS: I know what you went through. We went through twelve years of it with our daughter, only to just now find out what we kept trying to tell the school, that D. never should have been placed in their special classes. She is a beautiful, sweet, shy girl who knows and understands the schools' mistake. She is angry. We are angry also. She has gone through so many years of misery, loneliness, and fears. We had her tested, spent hundreds of dollars here and there, and none of the tests told us anything, yet the schools demanded her placement in a Special Education class, to be mainstreamed into a regular class later on. *Later on never came.* We found a tutor for D. and after one year, she passed a regular math class in spite of many teachers who told her to her face she could never do it. She passed! She will graduate this year. I only wish we could have been stronger and made them leave her alone.

N.H. OF MADISON, WISCONSIN: I won an award from the California Psychological Association in 1973 for my study concerning the best classroom structure of educationally handicapped children. I know you are correct when you suspect that government funding has increased the number of EH kids. And to the emotional and educational detriment of many children. . . . I've worked with all sorts of kids who were slotted to "fail" because they were a designation and not a person. EH is a big money-making business.

K.B. OF TROY, MICHIGAN: We struggled through a similiar ordeal, while all the time wondering why our son P., now age eighteen, had been tagged "special" by teachers and psychologists. At age seven, he was given a battery of tests and placed in Special Education under the classification of "emotionally disturbed." He spent many unhappy years in Special Ed classrooms, where he was labeled a retard and taunted by others which, of course, resulted in a poor self-image and painful shyness. I questioned the decisions and testing methods of these so-called educators and learned social workers, often storming out of parent-teacher meetings in tears, frustrated with the condescending manner in which they were conducted. Finally in ninth grade, after a lot of help from private tutors and a psychologist, P. was able to pull himself out of Special Ed. He will graduate next year, possibly with honors.

M.P.M. OF PHENIX CITY, ALABAMA: Your story is the story of my grandnephew. The abuse that this child has suffered at the hands of a Special Education teacher would be criminal if a parent administered it. I thought ours was an isolated case but it is not.

V.P. OF WAIALUA, HAWAII: We enrolled our child in a Catholic school. Let me say they have not changed their Gestapo methods since I was a student in the fifties. Our son didn't color outside of the lines—he colored a gorilla blue! He was seen as hopelessly uneducable, of course. I could go on and on, but it is enough to say that K. has blossomed at an excellent Montessori school. I hope your experiences help enlighten at least one parent of a small late-bloomer. Different is better in many ways and should not be labeled Special Ed.

C.V. OF NILES, ILLINOIS: I am from Yugoslavia. I came to the United States to escape the Nazis. It is like the Nazis now here, what they are doing to the children. A psychologist tested my son. He said to me, "I know you Croatians, on the South Side of Chicago. You like to knock your kids around. You too hard on them." I have nothing to do with South Side. To me, this is a prejudiced man against me. They tell me my son needs help, I say all right. The Americans know about children, I think. They are experts. I gave them my son into Special Education. He is in Special Education class for five years and he learns nothing. When he starts he is reading at second-grade. After five years, he is reading less. He is illiterate. I talk to the teacher, he says these kinds of kids you let them do whatever they want, no use to teach them. They roller-skate in school, they make cookies, they teach kids nothing. I hate it. My son hates it. The others call him "retard." He tells me once he is locked in a dark closet all day. I say this cannot be true. I go to school and they say it is true. They tell me, "Your son is retarded." I tell you, my head splits. I am mad. Then they say, no, he is not retarded, he is behavior-disordered. For five years, they say he is a good boy, now they say he is disordered. They say he must go to youth campus full-time. I fight for him. They say my home is a bad environment for him. I fight them and spend all my money and the state says I am right, but the school district says they will give "diagnostic placement" and put him in youth campus next year. I am going bankrupt now and I have saved my son because I put him in high school in Boys Town in Nebraska. My house is being sold for all my debts. I ask you this: Why did this happen to my son, to me?

P.C. OF MESILLA, NEW MEXICO: My son's fourth-grade teacher called me in and told me she would like some tests run. The consultation at the school with the principal, the teacher, and the tester will remain with me until I die. The tester was a graduate student from the University of New Mexico, who informed my husband and I that the tests showed that C. was borderline retarded—certainly no more than a "dull normal." I will never forget or forgive the way the tester smirked when she pronounced the evaluation. It was not the school's fault that he could not read, and that was all they cared about. There is no greater evil in this world than what those people did to me and to my son that day. I cannot forgive myself for believing them. Much of my hopes for my son died then, and for the next several years

I treated C. with kindness but with a great hollowness of feeling. I felt his future must be one of small expectations, and we had another young boy—one of such astounding sparkle and talent that he did indeed make his brother look very limited. The school began to have Special Education classes and C. was put there. There was a special cement-block closet that the students were put in when their behavior was too violent. C. was given the same repetitive math workbook semester after semester, and as long as he was quiet no one cared what he did. Then I went to "open house" at school for my youngest son's first grade and, again, my world collapsed. They had placed him in the lowest section—with those who were later to be evaluated for "special" placement. Some part of me burst apart. They were wrong about this child and if they were so wrong about this one, they were wrong about the dullness of the other one. What could I have done when C. was being taught to consider himself a "dummy"? Knowing what I know now, I would do two things differently. One, I would never begin to even entertain the thought that the school and those terribly evil tests were right. That evaluation caused irrecoverably lost years in my relationship with C. Two, I would fight the entire school system to have him taken out of school completely. There is no place for people like C. in the schools. The solutions and special placements are vastly destructive. Permanent damage is done in the programs that basically just make jobs for Special Education teachers.

(The last two cases cited above are typical. Again and again, we have found that foreign-speaking parents or children who bear ethnic names or, especially, black kids are singled out for Special Education placement. And it is very usual for a school system to place brothers and sisters of kids already in Special Ed in the same programs, for no other reason than that there is a vague feeling that learning disabilities run in families or that families with "different" children must be substandard.)

R.N. OF BENTON HARBOR, MICHIGAN: After seventeen years of teaching in the public schools in Michigan, I had more than enough. I was not only very concerned about the grouping of special children in what you term "dummy rooms," but was appalled at the number of children who were screened into Special Education on the basis of the recommendation of teachers or an Intermediate School District psychologist. On more than one occasion, I was involved in a prescreening conference or screening conference to select new Special Ed students and wondered, what if the test is wrong? I disliked the fact that many Special Education teachers would mainstream special children whom the Special Ed teacher *could not control*. You have hit the nail of this problem on the head.

K.H. OF ROCHESTER, NEW YORK: Let me tell you about the son of my next-door neighbor. I am in Special Education as a speech therapist. I have watched this boy grow up and had no special concerns about him. I try to watch children develop whether I am teaching or not. After his kindergarten year, his mother told me that they were going to leave the boy back (in kindergarten) or put him in a class for the retarded. She was terrified. I tested him and found the boy had about a three-year delay in his hand-eye coordination, but otherwise he was fine. In speech and language development, he was above his chronological age. So I went with his mother to the school and set out to do battle with the Rochester school system. We refused a kindergarten placement for him and insisted that he be put into first grade with resource-room support. I thought this would settle the matter. It didn't. When the school opened in the fall, I was shocked to find out that the boy had been placed in, of all things, a bilingual classroom! This boy is not of Hispanic descent and he had never before heard Spanish! Yet here he was in a class where Spanish was spoken for half the day. So we fought again and, because my time is limited, I have since trained the boy's mother to fight for her child's rights and things are going better.

B.MCC. FROM ATLANTA, TEXAS: Our son R. had childhood dyslexia. I use "childhood" for want of a better term. When he began school in the mid-sixties, no one in our school system, much less our small town, had ever heard of this malady.

Parents have strange intuitions and secret knowledge about their children. We know them better than anyone else. No one has to tell us when something is not quite right with them or their world.

We also had our fill with the professional world of education—the people who believe that they and they alone know what is best for the child who walks to the beat of a different drummer.

Had we not taken the educational bull by the horns, stomped on toes, made all sorts of racket, and placed R. in a private school for three years, our son would not be the aerospace engineer that he is today. Had we gone along with our school system, R. would have been tracked into a slow-learners' group, ending up in a trades class in high school.

Hang in there. Believe in yourself and in Alec. Continue to walk with him to the beat of his drummer. Listen closely. If you haven't heard the sound of the beat yet, you will. What a sweet sound—what a sweet sound!

C.T. FROM PALATINE, ILLINOIS: My son J. was evaluated by a contractual psychologist, who I now know handles an unbelievable caseload. . . . The psychologist's recommendation was to hold J. back in first grade, not because of academic levels, but for lack of social maturity. The psychologist said, "Consider when J. is in high school. Many of his peers will reach puberty before him, growing pubic hair before him. They will be dating before him and taking driver's education before him. J. then will feel socially and physically immature." Keep in mind we were supposed to be talking about a boy who is only six years old! . . . I disagreed totally with everything they said about my son. It was as if they were talking about someone else's child. I was never informed of any other alternatives or that I was entitled to any kind of rights. . . . He still has bad memories of the psychologist who evaluated him, and so do I. It took J. a long time to forgive me for putting him through the nightmare. I no longer get "on his case" to read and do his homework, and he works well under less pressure. I do, however, spend an enormous amount of time on being with him. We share lots of fun times, I'm enjoying his childhood with him and teaching him the most important subject of all, *love*.

I.L., ESCANABA, MICHIGAN: Our son M. is profoundly deaf with serious impairment as well. Luckily our first oral-deaf teacher was a caring, determined person who gave her very best for her students. . . . Her successor I soon found neither understood nor cared about deaf kids, so we pulled M. out of the program and put him in regular classes. We worked morning, noon, and night at home from first grade through junior college. Some regular teachers were cooperative, but others resented M. or had the "he should be put with his own kind" attitude. . . . Teachers sometimes made stupid remarks, the classic being that M. shouldn't take chemistry because if there were an explosion he wouldn't hear it! M. succeeded, not because of most teachers, but in spite of them. A few instructors deserve high praise. . . .

I'm so glad you persisted until you released Alec from that dirty label, and especially glad you went public with it. Perhaps it will help the thousands of mislabeled kids and those who truly are handicapped to get a more fair deal.

E.M., GOBLES, MICHIGAN: We are presently home-schooling our seven-year-old and five-year-old. We will continue this until we find a more viable alternative.

Our seventeen-year-old daughter, who will graduate next year, is a product of the public schools and I am proud to say that she has, thus far, survived it. Yes, I use the word *survive,* and I use that word with little pride. She learned how to play the game, how to get by. There was a great internal potential that was not tapped. . . .

So, with our next two, with much study, we have decided to opt for something other than the public schools. Living in a rural area, our choices of schools are limited. So we have a tutor come to our home and we also spend a great deal of time with our children. Our younger children are also involved in outside activities such as ballet, Sunday school, library class, play time with other children, etc.

Since home-schooling, I have learned that learning is ongoing. It is a natural instinct for a child to learn. But not all learn at the same pace. And what is even nicer is that I have had time to learn with and from my children!

I would like to share with you something I finally learned to do when our oldest was in early grades. I would go to the fifteen-minute conferences where I was quickly inundated with all that our daughter was doing which she was not supposed to be doing. When I was finally able to overcome my own feelings of inferiority with the school system, I would listen to all the negatives and then say, okay, now tell me something good about this child. Some of the looks on teachers' faces showed that they were floored to have a parent sit there and demand to hear some good qualities about their child. Believe me, it worked wonders!

What most letters illustrate are three principles for parents who want to get a good education for their kids and don't want their kids labeled or ignored.

1. *Fight hard and early.* Parents don't fight because they don't want to rock the boat and get the system down on their child. What they don't understand is that once the system decides to label a child, they are already down on him.

2. *Be prepared to fight for a long time.* School systems have time and money. If they don't get you to agree to labeling at first, they will try and try again. They try to wear you down, believing at some point you will simply give up the fight. Too many parents do and their children suffer for the rest of their lives. Children are too precious to abandon to an indifferent school system and a corrupt bureaucracy that has turned a noble idea—Special Education—into something that is truly evil.

3. *Remember that in the long run, time can be your ally.* A child needs twelve years in the school system in which to grow and learn. The more time you give him, the closer you both come to the time when he will be free of the system.

13

The New Segregation

This is a chapter for black parents in particular. Black children are more likely to end up in Special Education than white children.

No one in Special Education can argue with the facts. They don't try to for a simple reason: There is a widespread belief in Special Education circles that black children are more likely to be retarded, emotionally disturbed, or brain-damaged than white children. They are making Special Education—with its separate classes, separate school buildings, separate busing systems, and a separate watered-down education program—into the new school segregation.

A lot of the things now written or spoken about blacks originated in the Lyndon Johnson administration. Black people were socially inferior, they lagged behind white kids in school, there had to be special programs to help blacks catch up—Operation Head Start was just one of the do-gooder ideas that ultimately was used to do bad.

When we first isolated a suburban school district with a high percentage of black kids in Special Education, we were shocked by the reaction of teachers and school officials. We pointed out that in the school district, 7 percent of the black kids in high school were classified as educable mentally retarded—compared with a frequency rate most experts say should be around 1 percent nationally.

We got this amazing response signed by two seniors at a Chicago area teacher's college. They said they were going to be Special Education teachers: "The township [written about] includes the suburbs of A, B, and C. These are very poor areas and the prevalence rate of mild mental retardation is significantly higher in areas that do not nurture a stimulating environment or where mothers do not receive proper prenatal care and nutrition."

The suburbs mentioned were, in fact, middle-class in terms of income, average home cost, et cetera. But the suburbs were also predominantly black. What the two white Special Education teachers-to-be were saying was part of the coded jargon used in Special Ed today: Black people have inferior kids and need to be separated into special programs.

If we said black children are inherently inferior to white children, we would be bigots. But this sort of bigotry passes as education science once it is decorated with phrases that suggest black children are at high risk for mild retardation, neurological defects, and emotional disabilities because of pathological, psychosocial syndromes affecting the black family. Black children are being taught to be failures in droves.

As researcher James E. Ysseldyke of the University of Minnesota and some colleagues have discovered: "Many more minority students are being served in special education programs for the mildly handicapped than would be expected solely on the basis of the proportion of minority students in the general school population. This disproportion or overrepresentation is neither a new discovery nor an isolated practice, and it appears to hold especially for black children."[1]

There have always been more black children in school classes for the retarded than whites. There is considerable belief the reason for this is the bias in the IQ tests. Most educators will acknowledge that the IQ tests have a bias against blacks and other children whose cultural experience differs substantially from that of the average white child.

In 1972, in a California court case, the court ordered some eleven thousand black children reclassified because they had been channeled into classes for the retarded almost entirely on the basis of IQ test results. The court in that case based its finding on the fact that black parents demonstrated that while blacks constituted 28.5 percent of all students in the schools, 66 percent of the children in classes for the educable retarded were black.

Current national figures show blacks make up 16 percent of the students in this country—but they account for 39 percent of the educable mentally retarded population! And experts in the field believe that a similar overrepresentation of black children is a major trend in the fast-growing categories of learning disabilities and emotional disturbance.[2]

"The proportion of blacks in classes or training programs for the mentally retarded is two to three times higher than the proportion of white pupils in such classes and programs," a 1985 report prepared for the U.S. Department of Education concluded. "The proportion of blacks in classes or schools for seriously emotionally disturbed students is higher by two-thirds to three-quarters than the comparable proportion of whites. By contrast, the proportion of blacks in programs for the gifted and talented is 40 to 50 percent *lower* than the proportion of whites in such classes."[3]

Despite the bias built into IQ tests, they are still used to test black children, and educators pooh-pooh the cultural differences. After all, debate about the flaws in the IQ test has been going on since it was invented in 1904. Besides, even if you could create a fair IQ test for blacks and whites, there would be a way around it. As Ysseldyke and his colleagues said: "We contend that even if an agreement regarding what constitutes test bias could be reached and a test or set of tests that was completely nonbiased could be developed, there is no way to ensure that such a measure would be used fairly. Students may be deemed eligible for special education services even when no hard evidence exists to support such a placement."[4]

In other words, even if you passed an IQ test, Special Education testers could find something else wrong with you—perhaps your home life or the way you talk street jive.

Psychotesters always say they use more than the IQ test to decide to place a child in a class for the retarded. We have found that a child is placed in Special Education based on three factors: his IQ test, the teacher's evaluation of him, and his previous placement (if he was once labeled retarded, then the label sticks).[5]

It is the same fraud that Dr. Goddard pulled when he had his workers pick out mental deficients among immigrants streaming into Ellis Island based on the workers' intuition. If you think someone is retarded, then he is. If someone looks retarded to you, then he is.

If you think this is too harsh, you still don't understand how sick and corrupt the Special Education system has become. For example, when we wrote a brief account of our Special Education testing experiences in *Reader's Digest,* we received a number of letters from psychologists who said that our son should have been placed in a segregated classroom regardless of his IQ test scores, simply based on the judgment of the first-grade teacher who wanted to put him there! Even if the tests don't show retardation, teachers know best by intuition!

And a lot of white teachers believe in their hearts that

black kids are just inferior. And so the widespread and painful process of true school desegregation has been halted in the fastest-growing business in education—Special Ed. A teacher does not have to justify placing black Johnny or Jennifer in Special Education. It is, after all, for the child's own good.

Teachers can place kids in segregated classes once they find that the behavior of the kids is "different." Black kids are different. So are Hispanic children. American Indian children don't fit in and children of immigrants frequently have difficulty speaking well. Children who stutter do not fit in, children who are shy do not fit in, children who learn to read slowly do not fit in, and children who read too early do not fit in. And in every case, there is something wrong with the child—not the teacher and not the school.

A parents' group in Chicago, which has protested that more than seven thousand children may have been improperly placed in Special Ed classes for the retarded, found that black children were twice as likely to be put in such classes as white children. They were much more likely to be in full-time segregated programs. The part-time resource programs for Chicago children called learning-disabled, however, were more likely to be filled with white children.

"Those programs in which black students were over-represented in 1979–80 (Educable Mentally Handicapped and Educationally Handicapped) provided special education services almost exclusively in separate classrooms and schools. In contrast, those programs in which black students were under-represented provided special services either in the regular classroom or through part-time resource programs that allowed children to spend most of their time in the regular classroom," their report, *Caught in the Web*, concluded. The small number of cases where Special Education children were mainstreamed, consultants to the Chicago school district reported, involved more white children than black.[6]

This is not a problem exclusive to Chicago. This kind

of treatment is common in school districts across the country. The practice of putting minority children in segregated Special Education classes while white children with similar problems remained in the regular classroom with part-time resource help has been documented in a number of school systems.

Fact: About 80 percent of all kids labeled retarded have no physical ills to show diagnosticians a cause of the retardation. (And many kids who are thought to have physical "etiologies" or causes of retardation are victims of misdiagnosis. One father told us of his son, now a law school graduate, who was once diagnosed by a very confident medical team as hopelessly retarded because of a "pituitary gland burnout" that turned out to be nonexistent!)

Then how is retardation measured? Very imprecisely. Generally, kids called retarded are at the bottom of the ladder that allegedly measures intelligence. Some people are smart, some are dumb, no one can argue that. But when does it turn out that Johnny is smart? When he is eight or eighteen?

There are safeguards experts have identified that would reduce black overrepresentation in Special Education programs. One group has suggested that no child should be referred to the psychotesters for Special Education placement until three different teaching approaches have been tried with him. We know that this is not being done when many children are being referred to testing during their first or second week in kindergarten or first grade.

And there are special questionnaires and inventories aimed at getting from parents a real description of the child's out-of-school behavior. Where these have been used honestly, it's been found that the proportion of black children judged retarded shrinks to around 1 percent.

But this is rarely done—educators prefer to rely on the old standbys, the IQ tests and the teachers' judgments. There are many school districts in this country that place more than 10 percent of their black students in classes for the retarded. So why are a lot of black kids in Special Ed classes? Well, it's because a lot of black kids are dumb. That is the view of the psychotester who believes in his ability to measure intelligence.

In fact, most educators and psychologists view "mild" retardation as caused by substandard families. And we all know who the substandard families are, don't we? Families are examined to see if they are different from the other families in the school.

We have seen instances where children with ethnic last names going to school in white, Protestant, and very Anglo-Saxon areas suddenly are discovered to be in need of Special Education because of an indefinable something—a spot of difference—about them.

Black educator Marva Collins, who has struck out at the myth that black kids can't learn, says:

> Too often teachers, school psychologists and social workers have preconceived notions about children and pigeonhole them accordingly. Children with divorced parents run a high risk of being stereotyped, as do children from wealthy families, or those with working mothers, and black children living in neighborhoods like Garfield Park [a poor black section of the Chicago ghetto]. Tell some people where these children live, and right away they assume that the children are abused or neglected, that they come to school hungry, have no clothes, and have never lived with a father. Some teachers assume that these children can never learn anything.[7]

Deviance from the norm is the key to understanding the insidious nature of the new segregation. A recent study of black children whose families moved from the inner city of Chicago to the suburbs found that 6 percent of the black kids were in Special Education in the city, but in the suburbs 19 percent of them became eligible for Special Education. They were the same children, but somehow, during the move into white suburbs, they had acquired learning disabilities, emotional diseases, and retardation.[8]

Should a child from an upper-middle-class family achieve a low IQ score, chances are there will be more research done on his problem and he will earn a learning-disabled label or an emotionally disturbed classification. In Special Education journals, some educators argue that the label is not the important thing since the treatment in Special Education is always the same, so teachers should use labels on middle-class kids that sound more pleasing to middle-class ears.[9] A black child who scores low may not have that potentially troublesome middle-class family to fall back on, and the label of retarded is given more routinely.

Robert B. Edgerton, an expert on retardation at the Neuropsychiatric Institute of the University of California School of Medicine, explains the different kinds of retardation—as the experts see it:

> It is important to note that clinically retarded children are born to people of all social classes and ethnic groups. . . . Sociocultural retardation accounts for the remaining 75 to 80 percent of retarded individuals. It involves a mild intellectual impairment, with IQs ranging from 55 to 69. The condition is not diagnosed until the child enters school, has academic difficulties, and undergoes psychological assessment. There are seldom any marked physical handicaps and laboratory tests for physical abnormalities are usually negative. Such children are most likely to be born to parents who are economically, socially and educationally disadvantaged. . . .[10]

Naturally, parents of children who seem to have nothing wrong with them except a low test score get resentful when the educators want to call their child retarded and put him in a special segregated classroom. This, in turn, upsets people like Edgerton: "Parents of socioculturally retarded children often refuse to accept the label, and some become antagonistic to the school system as well as to the psychological testing that led their child to be called 'retarded' and set apart from other children.''[11]

In other words, parents of kids who don't act retarded as far as the parents are concerned resent some psychologist or graduate school exam-giver calling their kid retarded. Who can blame them? Besides Special Educators, of course.

The whole of public education in the United States is tottering because of the grave damage done to it by Special Education and the way Special Education systems are used to discriminate against colors, classes, and "different" groups of people. Johnny can't read, can't write, can't figure, can't think—and the education establishment spends billions of dollars every year to say that it is all Johnny's fault.

We don't think it is. We think there is something morally corrupt at the heart of the education system today.

Dr. Gerald Coles, asking why testing and labeling of children has increased so spectacularly in the last decade, declared in the *Harvard Education Review*: "By positing biological bases for learning problems, the responsibility for failure is taken from the schools, communities, and other institutions and is put squarely on the back, or rather within the head, of the child. . . . It is a classic instance of . . . blaming the victim."[12]

Public education is making a fool of itself defending indefensible practices concerning labeling kids and not teaching kids the things they need to know to achieve fulfillment in a complex world.

The IQ test stands at the heart of the system of segregation and discrimination. It has been used for this purpose since its invention.

Slowly but surely, we are creating an underclass of children who are conditioned to failure and who believe that failure is an acceptable life-style. They can't read—but someone will always be around to read to them. They can't function independently—so they will become lifelong dependents. This is a tragic waste of human life for the sake of ensuring a few more jobs in an educational growth industry.

Walter Lippmann, in a famous article in *The New Republic* in 1922, wrote against the IQ test and foresaw how the school system would come to lean on it to explain the system's failure: "If a child fails in school and then fails in life, the school cannot sit back and say: You see how accurately I predicted this. Unless we are to admit that education is essentially impotent, we have to throw back the child's failure at the school, and describe it as a failure not by the child but by the school."[13]

Unfortunately, we have enshrined failure in our school systems and we worship at the shrine every day in every Special Education classroom in the country, where too many poor and black and Hispanic children are taught to believe they are dependents of society and will be treated as dependent children all their lives. Black and Hispanic family life is denigrated routinely by education professionals, and this undermines the power of minority parents to defend their children against experimentation in the education establishment.

Lest white parents feel the problems do not affect them, listen to our cautionary tale. We were white, middle-class parents in the suburbs—and it happened to us as well. It is happening all over the country but particularly, at first, to minority parents. Experimentations in social tinkering carried on first among minorities eventually spread to the rest of the society.

PART FOUR

The Magic Feather

14

How to Save
Your Child

The struggle against a misguided bureacracy is not easy and it is long. In the previous section, we have tried to show that parents who do not think their children should be placed in Special Education programs—or who feel their child has been wrongly diagnosed as learning-disabled or otherwise handicapped—face a monumental struggle in getting a good education for their Johnny or Jennifer.

This is the part of the book in which practical alternatives in education are suggested—as well as teaching strategies we believe have resulted in improvement in kids *outside* of the Special Education structure. We hope parents can use this section as a resource with which they can take charge of their child's educational destiny—and ensure that he gets the best of care without labels.

First, there are some obvious alternatives.

If your child is slow in some subject area at school—and you have the money or time—tutor him privately. This means you can hire a private teacher to work in a one-on-one situation with the child to improve his skills. This method works frequently and works well. Why? Because the private tutor is usually oriented toward getting results. After all, that is what he (or she) is paid for. The private tutor has no incentive to prove that a child *cannot succeed.* A private tutor is not after government funding for a Special Education program and does not have to show that Johnny or Jennifer is slow in returning to normal—as many Special Education teachers in public schools admit they do.

But private tutors are not cheap. They have to make a living. They generally work one-on-one. This is time-consuming and expensive for them—and the parents.

People with less money can spend more time with Johnny or Jennifer. It is still not against the law in this country to teach your kids yourself.

Is Johnny having trouble reading? Sit down with him for an hour or a half-hour a day and work with him in the complex process of learning to read. See for yourself if you think your son has an eye or a hearing problem. Perhaps his school, like many, does not believe in the phonics method of teaching—though teaching reading through phonics is the easiest and surest way to get young kids to read. So pick up a book on teaching phonics and override the school system; teach Johnny yourself!

"I can't! I don't have time!" some parents tell us. They're pressed at the workplace and do not have the money or time to educate their children. They are the parents who surrender easily to the paraprofessionals and give up Johnny's future to dark days in Special Education where he learns to be a lifelong failure.

It is too bad such people ever decided to have children. Being a parent is a lifelong commitment. You never outgrow your responsibility to your child. He or she was born into this world because of you—not because of anything he or she did. In three years of talking with parents whose children have gotten a raw deal from the educators, we're surprised that so few are willing to fight or to teach their children themselves. It is difficult to understand why parents so casually give up their kids to strangers after going through the trouble—and pain and joy—of raising them for four or five years.

Some parents don't want to rock the boat by opposing recommendations of teachers or school psychologists or principals. They feel awkward in the position of middle-aged rebel. So did we. But remember that if you do not rock the boat at the beginning—when a bad diagnosis is presented to you—then it will become nearly impossible to correct the problem later. Bureaucracies are like undergrowth in the rain forests: They overwhelm those who merely stand still.

Some parents would rather abandon their kids to a wrong diagnosis in a corrupt educational system than be bothered with fighting. They are contemptible. They are not only cowards for themselves, their cowardly hesitation directly hurts their children.

Still other parents are confused when a teacher suddenly proclaims that Johnny shows evidence of "minimal brain damage" or Jennifer is "emotionally disturbed."

Join the club. Everyone is confused when, out of the blue, their child is singled out for a Special Education diagnosis. The bureaucracy is quick to move in the climate of confusion. School conferences are held, papers are to be signed, parent-teacher meetings are scheduled . . . and before you know it, Johnny has been certified as learning-disabled and marched off to the dummy class.

Don't be confused. Read this book from cover to cover. Learn to understand what Special Education is—and what it is not. If this book is only a beginning, turn to our recommended bibliography and find other books to help you with your problems.

Some of the most pathetic letters we received came

from parents who wrote to us asking for a name or an address that had just appeared in one of our articles. They were more willing to spend twenty-two cents on a letter to us—so that we could find the article, make a copy, and send it back to them—than to go to the local public library and look up the article themselves. Parents have to be resource people! It is not that difficult, and you do not need a college degree to be able to look things up in the local library.

A special note on your local public library: Librarians are pros. They know how to find information. They know how to get books, even books they may not carry at the moment. Libraries are famous for interlibrary cooperation and lending systems. We doubt there is an area in this country where the local library cannot serve as a fount of knowledge on the subject of Special Education—as long as the parent is interested enough to use the library. Armed with a library —and a sympathetic librarian—any parent can become an expert in Special Education in a matter of months—certainly as much of an expert as the average schoolteacher. You will often find that a teacher who has sounded quite confident in using pseudoscientific terms like *minimal brain dysfunction* will be struck dumb when you tell her what it really means. The chances are good she hasn't the faintest idea.

We are sorry to talk in terms of combat when suggesting ways to get the right education for your Johnny or Jennifer. Unfortunately, that is what it has been reduced to in many districts.

Perhaps your school district is the exception. If so, test them. When they recommend that your child be placed in Special Education, ask to see the special facilities, ask how many children (as a percentage) are in special facilities, ask about the curriculum that is going to help your child. And ask for the information in writing. If there is reluctance to answer, then they are hiding something from you. If you believe the curriculum is not going to help your child any more than leaving him in a regular classroom, say so and see what the response is. If you refuse to allow your child to be held back in class—and they are now holding back children to repeat kindergarten routinely in many districts —see what the response is. And then decide whether you have a fight on your hands.

Remember that nearly 12 percent of all kids in the country are now in Special Education, and thousands more are being added every year. If parents let the Special Ed factory grow at the rate it's been growing in the last few years, nearly a fifth of all our children will be in Special Education by the turn of the century—and that is only fourteen years away!

This madness has to stop, and we have to fight it. But that is not your first concern as a parent. Your concern is with one little boy or one little girl. Save him. Save her. Do it now. Nobody wants to fight—but sometimes the fight comes to you.

We intend to cram this section of the book with good, positive advice on a wide range of problems—problems with kids, problems with parents, problems with schools. We are going to start with typical questions from worried parents about what to do next.

Q. The school has suggested that our son have Special Education evaluation. Don't you think we ought to wait and see what the tests say before we decide what to do? We are somewhat interested in the results in any case, because we cannot understand why our son is having trouble in school.

A. First of all, we suggest you prepare yourself for bad news. It is rare for any child to be given a psychoeducational evaluation and come out with a clean bill of health. Further, understand that such testing is a drastic thing to do to a child—no matter how "painless" the testers say it is. Educators do not recommend such testing unless they want a "scientific" justification for placing the child in a different school environment.

Moreover, we have attempted to show in this book that the research into Special Education clearly shows that Special Education placement does no good for most of the children subjected to it and that the primary gain is for the teacher (who gets rid of a child she doesn't want to deal with) and the school district (that gets federal money). Does your son's teacher want to get rid of your son? Have you talked to her? Is she hostile toward your child? Does she make up stories about how many times he disrupts the class or fights with other kids?

At the moment, all you have to fight is the opinion of a teacher that your son is abnormal in some way, and that is why she is requesting an evaluation. After the tests are done and experts have written in their scores, the child will not have changed—*but you will find yourself in a much weaker position.* If you have read this book, you know—as the experts already know—that the test results are meaningless because the tests themselves are based on fraudulent research and faulty assumptions. Unfortunately, the laws of most states allow the educators to use these test results as if they were Holy Writ.

We happen to think that any parent in your position—unless they really and truly believe their child suffers from rare and severe medical abnormalities—ought to fight to avoid getting caught under the Special Education steamroller. And that is because the testing process itself—as we discovered—is very damaging to kids. "All children are sensitive to being thought of as 'different,'" writes optometrist and Special Educator Jerome Rosner. "Avoid excessive testing. Not only is it expensive in terms of time and money, it may also be demoralizing for the child."[1]

Special Educators know that all the tests can be terribly frightening to children, yet they continue to assure parents they are not harmful. Why? Because without tests you can't pretend it's all scientific, and you can't have labels. And what is important to the system is not the well-being of your child, but the label that can be attached to him.

The "diagnostic process" by which that label is attached is time-consuming and inevitably damaging to a child's self-esteem. In most districts it costs more than $2,000. And yet, it has been shown over and over that it rarely provides any information that will actually be used by a teacher to teach a child.

More news from the same front: We have received many letters from parents who felt their relationship with their children was damaged severely by Special Education tests—as well as by the Special Ed process that usually follows. Here is one heartbroken mother: "I know my son felt betrayed that I let them put him through this. How could I have known that this was going to permanently damage our relationship? I've spent the last year trying to make up for it and convince him again that he is loved for himself."

Q. Our son's teacher sends home notes about things he does wrong at school. Nearly every day we get a phone call or note about his use of bad language or inattention in class or misbehavior at recess. Most of the incidents do seem trivial. We have tried to tell her that she should put her foot down, that we do not tolerate this behavior at home. We are afraid she is just building up a case against our son. There is not much we can do, since we can't handle her discipline problems for her. We are considering calling for psycho-educational evaluation on our own, so the experts can tell her our son is normal and energetic and so that he will not be placed in some special program.

A. We've said it before and we'll say it again: Few testers are going to tell a teacher a child is normal and healthy. They aren't in the business of testing normal kids.

Have you talked to your son? Have you told him you don't want him to act up at school? Have you questioned him on each incident detailed in the phone call or note? What has been the result?

Dr. Rudolf Dreikurs, a psychiatrist, has written about what he calls "love letters" from teachers to parents about little Johnnies acting up:

It is a generally accepted practice to send such notes to the parents. Why? If you ask the teachers they will tell you that the parents want this information. But do the teachers always do what the parents want? Of course not. They will say that the parents ought to know. Why? Does the teacher really expect the parents to improve the situation? If the teacher is honest with herself she will know that nothing will change. . . . Then why does she send them? In our discussions it became quite clear. The teacher feels so defeated by the child in her class that she wants to cause a little trouble for him at home.[2]

Perhaps the teacher is inadequate. Despite the assurances of the National Education Association that all teachers are perfect, a lot of teachers have attained tenure by showing up on time and collecting a paycheck every two weeks.

Face facts: You and your son are being harassed. You ought to be keeping a record of every communication you have with this teacher, including time and date. Every note she sends should be answered immediately—*and send copies to the principal and the superintendent.* You should respond to all telephone calls with a written summary of your understanding of what the phone conversation was about, and send this to the teacher immediately and to the principal and the district superintendent as well.

Does this sound paranoid on our part? A panel for Illinois school board members specifically advised educators to leave a "paper trail" of complaints about a child the teacher wishes to have diagnosed as abnormal and placed in Special Education. The "paper trail," they advised, will make it easier to fight parental complaints about the placement.[3]

There is a possibility that the teacher is not trying to place your son in Special Ed—she is merely a whiner. The school systems are full of them. Develop a thick skin about her complaints and try to talk to the principal about putting your son in another class—though principals are usually very reluctant to approve transfers of children from one class to another, because they don't want to go along with parental criticism of a teacher. Principals are generally impotent nabobs caught between the militant teachers (and their unions) and the purse strings held by the district superintendents.

Remember that a kid can have a bad teacher one year, but next year brings a different teacher who may not have the same attitudes. If that is not the case, you may have to consider alternative schooling—going to a private school. It is unfortunate that the once-proud public school system of this country is increasingly abandoned by people who have a chance to vote with their feet—who move to private schooling as a solution to escaping bad teachers and bad curricula in public schools.

Q. Our daughter's teacher wants us to sign a form to permit psychological testing. She is five and in kindergarten. We have refused, but there has been a lot of pressure on us to sign the consent forms. The principal calls us two or three times a week and tells us that our daughter needs to be tested. He says our daughter shows signs of being immature. All this pressure is making me a nervous wreck.

A. If you think you have pressure now, just imagine what it will be like after a few experts have been called in and allowed to decide scientifically that your daughter is either dumb, brain-damaged, or crazy—though the exact phrase will be much nicer.

You are being bullied and you don't know it. You are falling into the self-pity trap. In time, you will give up your daughter to make life easier on yourself. This is contemptible. Realize you are being bullied—and fight back. Don't take it; dish it out. Your daughter's future is at stake. Imagine your principal thinking your daughter is immature in kindergarten—what does he expect from a five-year-old?

Q. Our son was diagnosed as learning-disabled. We agreed to the diagnosis because he was having learning problems. But it seems to us that the resource-room help is not helping him. It is little more than baby-sitting and hand-holding.

The Special Education teachers seem to us to be encouraging our son to think of himself as being unable to solve his own problems. Everything is done for him. He is also missing a lot of schoolwork in his regular class and his regular teacher seems to be ignoring him.

At our last meeting with the school, the staff told us that our son is performing "commensurate with expectations" and that our goals for our son are unrealistic. How do we get out of this mess? Our son is falling behind.

A. Experts think the worst effect of part-time Special Education placement is the tendency of regular teachers to believe they are relieved of responsibility for the special child. If he doesn't learn in regular classes—well, it's because he's special, isn't it? It certainly has nothing to do with the teacher. Dr. Ysseldyke ran research that showed regular teachers are in such awe of Special Ed diagnosticians that they rarely even *speak at all* in meetings in which they supposedly are consulted on how to remediate a child's weaknesses.[4] The most silent members of the evaluation team are usually the people who know the child—the teacher and the parents.

Meanwhile, Special Education works its trap—a special child becomes part of a self-fulfilling prophecy of failure. The regular teacher no longer thinks of the child as her student—and in order to go work on his self-esteem or his perceptual training or whatever in the resource room, he is missing valuable class time. Thus it is precisely the students who are having academic problems who end up getting the least academic instruction! Special Educator Harry Chandler writes:

> The biggest problem [for Special Education teachers] now is that regular class teachers still resist working with special students, still haven't been trained to work with special students, and still send those students back to the Spe-

cial Education teacher for tests, homework, initial instruction, drill, and for discipline. Even in elementary schools where a classroom teacher has a special student for five and one-half out of six hours, the special teacher still gets children sent back with a note saying, "Take care of *your* student, I don't have time right now."[5]

You mention "hand-holding." A lot of parents use that word to describe Special Education instruction. Experts agree—they are noting increased examples of what they call "learned helplessness" among Special Ed kids. The kids absorb the idea that they are not in charge of their destinies, that some mothering bureaucracy will have to "do" for them because they cannot "do" for themselves. Surveys of time spent in Special Ed show that special children get overwhelming approval for very little achievement —and this confuses them and lowers their levels of expectations.

Yes, you and your child are in a "mess" as you describe it. And it will be a mess to get out of it.

First, go to the principal of the school and state your misgivings in plain English. At the same time, put everything in writing. Be friendly and firm. Often, educators will not fight parents who want to remove their children from part-time Special Ed placement—it isn't worth it because part-time placement generates little money for the school district from federal and state sources. (Yes, that sounds cynical, but money is what Special Education is about.)

What if they refuse? Unfortunately, you will then have to either remove the child from the public school—and try to get him into a private school that may want to go along with the Special Education placement—or consult an attorney. But act fast. Things will not get better. Your son is suffering right now.

A note on attorneys: Few attorneys are instructed in the intricacies of education law. Fewer are willing to take cases from parents who want to stop Special Education from interfering with their child's education. You should consult your local bar association first. Talk to other parents. Groups like the Association for Children with Learning Disabilities might be able to help on this. Find out if there is an attorney known to fight for parents', and kids', rights. You might try your local chapter of the American Civil Liberties Union for advice—though the ACLU has not shown much eagerness in challenging the vast Special Education program and the attendant placement laws in this country. *However,* and this is a major point, *school board attorneys will generally say they have never lost a Special Education case.* This is nonsense. Parents can sue for a proper education for their children and courts can rule in favor of parents. Parents need a dedicated attorney, and they are not that easy to find.

Q. I want to confess a terrible mistake. When my son was three and slow to talk, I called the Special Education district and asked them to put him in a program for special kids. They did. It was terrible—really horrible. He was bused for nearly two hours a day, he was exhausted when he came home, and he picked up bad behavior from the other kids.

Two years ago, when he was five, they tested him at school and said he was retarded. This was the beginning of the nightmare for us. He was in an EMH program for a year and I worked actively with the school—even to taking the class on outings and so forth. I realized at the end of the year that my son did not belong in this class. I fought to have him retested, and when he was retested he scored in the normal range on the IQ test. And then the teacher told us she knew my son was not retarded the first week of school—but she didn't say anything!

Now the district refuses to place him back into a regular class. They say because he still speaks slowly he is now a "behavior-disorder" case. We think this new diagnosis is insane, because he is a sweet, quiet child who has never been reported as a problem in class. I looked at the program they've suggested—it's a separate school—and it is clearly designed for violent or aggressive children. We can't see how such a placement could do our son anything but harm.

Since our district has already admitted they misdiagnosed my son in the first place, don't they owe me some real help to undo the damage they have done? I want him in a regular class. I know he could do the work if he gets the chance. I am just heartsick about this.

A. Misdiagnosis is supposed to be illegal. However, the requirements of the state and federal bureaucracies that fund Special Education programs are lax. If the school district filled out the required paperwork—well, you can write to your senator but don't expect much more than a statement of sympathy.

You need a lawyer right now. Do you really want to keep your child in a school system as incompetent as the one you describe? In a number of cases, parents have forced school boards to pay private school tuition by going to court on the matter.

Meanwhile, teach your son now and love him and respect him. Don't let the horrible experiences he has undergone destroy his faith in himself. If the worst scenario is played, take him out of school, keep him home, and teach him yourself. You may be able to work with other parents who are doing the same thing. You should make a point of talking to people about your problems in education. We were surprised to find out how many people were in the same situation we were, and in some cases sharing ideas, energy, and time was tremendously useful.

We realize these are not pat answers. Well, this subject of Special Education is not the stuff of advice columns in the daily papers.

Q. I agreed to have my son evaluated. However, reading about the tests, I decided that they were using at least one that was very, very questionable. It is a sort of "personality inventory" and it is sold to schools by a commercial company and it is supposed to be "validated" by being used on a large number of children. Results of that test show my son is hyperactive and probably emotionally disturbed. When I objected to this test because it takes a teacher's judgments and makes them scientific truths, the school said I did not understand the complexity of design in this sort of test.

A. *You made the mistake of trying to beat the testers at their own game.* The tests may be quite wonderful statistical instruments, but if they are administered in a ham-handed fashion or interpreted to mean more than they can possibly mean, they are wrong.

Wrong is a five-letter word that applies to most of the testing procedure used to shovel kids into Special Education programs in public schools. You can spend your life— and your child's life—quibbling over correlation coefficients. The Special Educators would certainly be happy to accommodate you if you want to argue with them about test results, rather than hear you question the whole faulty process of psychodiagnosis.

Gerald Coles, after reviewing the ten tests most widely used to diagnose learning disabilities, concluded that their use was not defensible. "There is little question that eventually the tests reviewed here will be discarded: the evidence against them is mounting," he wrote. "The central question is really whether recognition of the invalidity of these tests will result in abandonment of an untenable professional dogma, or whether it will merely result in the test battery being replaced by other equally questionable instruments."[6]

Well-qualified researchers have demonstrated over and over that the tests educators use simply cannot make the distinctions between children that they want to make. If educators cling to this faulty procedure in the face of hard evidence, it must be because the educators' need for scientific self-justification is greater than their respect for truth.

You are the only one who cares enough about your child to know his true situation. You can't abdicate your responsibility for his future by going along with the "experts" just because they use big words to fit small-minded diagnoses.

Q. My daughter is being blacklisted. She was identified last year as having a behavior problem in third grade. We know she is a handful, but we think the problem is with the school —she is bored by the pace of the curriculum. We are disillusioned with public school and would like to get her into a good private school with a rigorous academic program.

The problem is now that no such private school will take her. We have talked to people at two of them, and when we mentioned the problems she had in public school, they said they had no opening for her—even though I know they have openings.

A. More and more private schools cooperate with the public schools in a sort of informal blacklist of unwanted children. When a child transfers from a public school to a private school, his files go with him—and they can contain devastating and one-sided teacher evaluations. Even if you have a religious claim—a Catholic who wants to go to a Catholic school or a Lutheran to a Lutheran school—often the religious order running the school will reject your child if they think she might be a problem.

It isn't fair but it's the way things are. Most private schools are in the business of making money as easily as possible—not helping problem kids or kids perceived as potential problems. And your attitude toward your daughter also puts *you* on the blacklist—private schools do not want parents who are too activist.

You might consider keeping your child home and teaching her yourself. Sure it sounds tough—but would it be better for her to waste the next nine years of her life in mediocre school programs where she learns how to fail for the rest of her life? You might consider moving out of your school district. Or you might consider enrolling your daughter in a solid correspondence school like the accredited (and acclaimed) Calvert School in Baltimore, Maryland, which has elementary and secondary courses aimed primarily for children of U.S. citizens overseas. Your public school might oppose these moves—which is why you need an attorney right now.

Let's sum up some key points:

1. *Time is of the essence.* Your child is changing every day. You can't leave him in a hopeless school situation and hope things will get better. They won't. Don't kid yourself and don't kid your kid.

2. *Get a lawyer.* It is expensive and you might get the wrong lawyer but you have to make a start if you are going to fight an entire school system.

3. *Learn to be skeptical.* Parents are often fooled by fancy words and softball diagnoses from the educators. The truth is that Special Education isn't special and it isn't education. The truth is that nearly all kids segregated in special programs suffer from the programs. The truth is that nearly all the diagnostic tools used to peg a child are wrong, are based on fraudulent assumptions, and are part of the fabric of self-fulfilling prophecies that teach children to be failures.

4. *Keep records.* When you meet with principals or teachers, record the conversation. This is perfectly legal—and makes principals bent on bending the Special Education laws nervous. Keep a diary of contacts with teachers. When you get a note from a teacher, keep it and answer it in writing and make copies of everything. Remember that often the law is used to force acceptance by parents of a faulty Special Ed diagnosis. You will have to learn to use the law as well if you want to save your child. And if it comes to consulting a lawyer—or even suing your school district —all those records you kept will become useful evidence in any legal proceeding.

5. *Love your child.* Sometimes lost in all this advice, discussion, and argument is the reason for this book: love for your child. Love him; love her; fight for him or her; be willing to devote your life to see that your child grows up free, whole, and with great expectations of him- or herself and the world he or she enters. Love goes a long way toward assuaging the bitterness and discomfort of a long fight. Your kid will understand what you are doing for him, or her. Your kid needs you as a role model; be one.

It is quite true that any number of parents with children in Special Education programs see those programs as being beneficial to their kids—despite the evidence we have cited in this book. We presume those parents will not read this book. A lot of people are terribly smug about accepting faulty diagnoses and soothing notes from teachers. We can cite one case after another of children mislabeled by a corrupt system—and a lot of parents will say, "Well, that's true of all the cases you cited but it's not true in our case." Fine. If you are satisfied, there is no way we will rock your satisfaction. Just one last question: When your Johnny is twenty-two or twenty-three and finally free of the education trap you accepted so easily, will you ask him what he thought about your decision?

15

The Magic
Feather

Dumbo is an elephant in the circus. Dumbo is not like the other elephants. He has large ears and looks awkward and he is truly clumsy. The other elephants shun him.

One night, Dumbo—in his shame—becomes intoxicated by accident along with his friend, a mouse who lives on the fringe of the circus. After a long dream, Dumbo and the mouse awake from their intoxicated slumber to find they are on the branch of a tree. They are off the ground. How did they get there?

The mouse realizes immediately that Dumbo must have flown into the tree, using his gigantic ears as wings. He tells Dumbo this, but the elephant refuses to believe him. Dumbo is so convinced that he is a failure—all the other elephants have derided him because he is clumsy and because he looks different—that he now believes he can do nothing special. And it would be a special thing if he was an elephant who could fly.

At this point, a group of wisecracking, hip crows on a fence start deriding the elephant and the mouse. The mouse, in a rage, says that Dumbo can fly and that all he needs is a little confidence in himself to do this different thing that no other elephant can do.

One of the crows understands the problem and says to the mouse that he will give Dumbo a magic feather to give him the confidence to fly. He plucks the feather from the tail of another crow, cackles and winks, and says to the mouse: "You want to make the elephant fly, don't you? Well, you gotta use a lot of 'chology—you know, psychology. Now here's what you do—use the magic feather!"

The mouse catches on to the scheme. "The magic feather? Yeah, I got you." He calls to Dumbo. "Dumbo, look! Have I got it! The magic feather! Now you can fly!"

Dumbo grasps the feather in his trunk and flaps his giant ears and—wonder of wonders—he flies. As long as he has the feather, he can fly.

Finally, one night in the circus, while he is about to perform his flying trick, he drops the feather in midfall from a platform. The mouse frantically assures him that the feather was not magic at all, that it was a way of building up his confidence, that Dumbo could really fly on his own all along.

Just before they crash on the circus floor, Dumbo flaps his ears.

And Dumbo flies.

That is the scenario of the charming Walt Disney animated movie. We chose the theme as the title of this book—and, in particular, this section—because we believe that children with special problems need a magic feather to build up their confidence to do the special things they are capable of doing.

We do not believe that diagnosing a child as a failure

at the age of five or six does him any good at all. We believe that parents will have to take a stronger hand. Kids with special problems—and all of us from time to time—need a magic feather to boost our confidence and to allow us to see a way to overcome learning difficulties. It is tragic to condemn a child to a label and to a failing way of life at an early age, when it would be so much better to see the good in a child—no matter how awkward or peculiar—and help the child to overcome his own problem himself.

All elephants do not fly and all children do not learn in the same way, at the same time, with the same course of instruction. Children are magic; they are miracles given to the rest of us to see the miracle in life all around us. Miracles should not be bruised or damaged.

There have been a lot of negative things that had to be said in this book. We felt it was necessary to warn parents about the pitfalls of Special Education in the public school system. We knew it was necessary to educate parents to the terminology and history of Special Education so that they would know what the coming fight was all about.

Now we want to tell you about good things that happen in education—and that you can make happen. Also, we want to tell you some good things that are being done in the area of vision testing and development, and about some good schools with good and different approaches to teaching kids.

There are so many bad people around that we can become too disillusioned. There is still good news and we intend to share it with you.

First, there is the conclusion of our story about our son. In the spring of 1984, he was eight years old and had completed the equivalent of second grade in a Montessori school. At this writing, he is in fourth grade in another Montessori school. It is a wonderful school, full of inquiring children with bright outlooks, full of bright learning objects the children handle as reverently as toys.

Before we decided to go public with our story in 1984, we asked for an evaluation of our son's progress from his teacher. She was a young woman from India who gave us a written report stating that his language and math skills were at grade level. Finally, she wrote: "He has an inquisitive mind. He is a cooperative child; cheerful and sociable with peers. In the beginning, he was a difficult child to reach; it took a month or so before he trusted me as his teacher. Sometimes he will burst out with a shout for no apparent reason but with no otherwise disruptive behavior. I found working with him enjoyable."

This was from a regular teacher in a regular class in a regular private school. Sixteen months before this written report card, our son had been diagnosed as so severely retarded as to be uneducable and so emotionally disturbed that he was described by a psychologist as "holding on to the thin edge of reality."

What made the difference for him then? We did. We decided that the diagnosis was wrong because it was not based on any reality. We saw Special Education at work in our public school and we knew it did not work on the face of it. Later, when we heard horror stories from others about Special Education, we knew we had made the right decision.

No child enters school at age five believing he will fail. Failure has to be taught to him. Childhood is a time of magic and a time of learning as part of that magic. Children possess the magic feather instinctively. They can do anything. Anyone who truly wants to teach a child will make certain from the beginning that a child's faith in himself is never shaken. No one can really call himself a teacher without understanding and practicing this.

Truly outstanding educators say this in different ways —the idea is not original to us.

Maria Montessori, who developed a whole system of education from her experience teaching the "unteachable" slum children of Rome, spoke gently of children at the age of three offering "amazing revelations of the greatness of the human soul."

Or Marva Collins, the teacher who set up a school for black children in the Chicago ghetto that was to prepare slum kids for college, who told of her approach to children who had already been conditioned to failure: "Oh [she tells them] you are so bright, so bright. I can't believe no one ever told you what a bright child you are." And the children respond by being bright because she gives them back the magic feather.

A real teacher knows that no one ever taught anyone anything by telling him ahead of time that he could not learn it. That is what Special Education is all about. It is about learning failure. Yes, you can teach children about things, but if they have lost their faith in themselves, they will be unable to grasp it.

Turn to the next chapter for information on a child's most important teacher—you.

16

Parents Are
Teachers Too

All right. You are at the point we were at a few years ago. You have a weird kid. Maybe he has trouble seeing the blackboard, maybe he is awkward, maybe he is slow in speech. In other words, he is a problem to some teacher in your school and the school wants to quickly categorize him and dump him into the Special Education bin and forget about him.

We use the masculine pronoun because it is extremely likely that your problem child is a boy. Boys make up the vast majority in Special Education classes. Makes you suspicious of Special Education right away, doesn't it?

You have had it up to here with the schools and their smarmy testers and pseudopsychologists. You are going to take your kid out of school and teach him yourself.

The school is shocked. Educators warn against teaching your child yourself. You are not qualified. You don't have the required number of education courses to your credit. And—the usual line—you are too emotionally involved with your own child to be an effective teacher.

It amazes us how successful educators have been peddling that last line—as though objectivity when dealing with children was something desirable; as though compassion, sympathy, and love were to be withheld from children during the teaching process.

Yet even parents who have watched inept, smug, and downright stupid teachers mangle their children's first attempts at reading and writing have told us they are afraid to challenge the authority of the classroom. Keep in mind that the school, as we now have it, is a relatively recent invention. Parents traditionally were the first and prime teachers of children through history. And today they are still the main teachers—whether they want to believe it or not, whether they accept the responsibility or not.

The great failure of education for children with school-based problems is not a failure of science or technique. What kids need is teaching by a sympathetic adult with patience and caring—not more tests, not labels, not scientifically controlled reading vocabularies or more theories about "neural pathways."

Most children adjust to school some time in first grade. Most learn to "get along and go along" with a minimum amount of fuss. They are embarked on the twelve-year education track that usually leads to a high school diploma —something that qualifies you to work in the neighborhood McDonald's.

But twelve years of school is not necessarily twelve years of education. Everyone admits the American public school system, on the whole, stinks. It routinely churns out batches of kids who can't read, can't write, can't figure, know little or nothing of history or geography or the arts, and are totally unfit for the complex challenges of modern life.

So what if you get your troublesome Johnny or Jennifer to adjust to school? It is no guarantee that he or she is ever going to read a great novel or know where Paris is or be able to tell you what momentous thing happened in 1066.

You are a parent and, therefore, you are a teacher. You have to be. A teacher is not a person who knows everything and imparts knowledge to the ignorant; a teacher is a helper who tries to open up the idea of learning in a student.

All right. You are convinced the schools are going to ignore your child's education because of his "problems." What do you do next? You might hire a tutor if you have the money. You should investigate the idea by contacting your nearest college or university (they usually have lists) or parents' associations in your area.

If Johnny has trouble reading, a private tutor can often clear up the problem in a short amount of time—as long as you are there as well to provide backup and follow-up.

If Johnny has a short attention span, try to find out why. Does he have an eye problem? Does he have trouble hearing? Has he got into the habit of just goofing off when faced with the responsibility of listening to others? He may have trouble paying attention in school—but does he have trouble following a story on TV? In short, try to separate out the parts of Johnny's problems and see what causes them, and then work on curing them.

In our case, our son was essentially denied an education in the first grade. Yet, by the end of his second year in school, the teacher said he was at a normal level for a second-grader. Was it a miracle?

In a sense, it was. Children have miracles locked inside them. What they really need is a magic feather to help them believe in themselves and discover their potential.

That statement will be derided as starry-eyed romanticism by the squadrons of public school Special Educators, teachers, and psychologists—but it is really at the basis of the approach of some of society's most innovative teachers.

Teaching is a commitment—not a job. And parents as teachers are going to have to decide in the beginning that their children can learn if they are taught, and that one way or the other, they are going to be taught.

In our case, our kitchen became the classroom and the kitchen table became the work desk between teacher and student.

How do you teach?

One goal at a time.

Take Johnny's alleged dyslexia. He can't tell *b* from *d.* The fact that many first-graders have this problem does not make many teachers less hysterical. It is seen as a sign of brain damage. Nonsense. Set one goal. This month Johnny will learn the difference between *b* and *d.* This month you set out to see why Johnny has this problem and what there is inside Johnny that will help him work it out.

We cannot praise enough Jerome Rosner or his book, *Helping Children Overcome Learning Difficulties.* He takes the approach that all children can learn—and that giving kids a label does not do much to help them learn. On the specific problem of teaching Johnny the difference between *b* and *d,* he suggests this approach:

> Underline with blue pencil every b in the child's reader. Point out to the child that the pencil is blue—stress the B sound. Do not mark the d in any way. A single hint is fine. As soon as there are two—one for the b and one for the d —the child is faced with the problem of keeping the hints straight.
>
> You may think it unreasonable to suggest that someone take the trouble to underline every b in the child's reader, but is it? If this is an effective way of helping to eliminate a major source of confusion, and if a simpler way cannot be invented, then it is not so unreasonable.[1]

Think about Rosner's quiet, patient approach to a single problem. There's a sort of beauty to it, don't you think?

All right, you say, that's a good approach to solving a problem but it does not solve the underlying neurological problem, does it? Wouldn't it be better to have an expert who knows the cause of these things work on correcting them at the source?

We are trying to persuade you that there is no "expert" who knows the true cause of such common educational hangups as letter reversals. They talk about the causes but they don't know what they are—and any honest researcher will tell you that. There are plenty of theories and a few techniques that sometimes work in some cases, but not in every case. Your Johnny or Jennifer is an individual, as different from others as his or her fingerprints.

It has been shown over and over that children with reversal problems do not see in reverse—but some teachers still won't buy it. Why? Because it is easier to write that Johnny is brain-damaged and send him off to Special Ed than think out some of the simple ways to help him overcome this one problem.

Rosner writes,

> There is no such thing as mirror vision. Certainly there are children who display what is termed persistent reversal tendencies, writing b's for d's and reading *was* for *saw.* But these children *do not see backward.* As noted before, they are simply persisting in a bad habit that they acquired at an earlier time in their life and never overcame. This is the only sensible way to view reversal tendencies; surely it is the only way that leads you to sensible methods for remediating the situation—helping the child replace the "bad" habit with the "good" one.[2]

Now that one problem has been demystified for you, let's consider another. The main problem our son had in learning arithmetic in the first grade appeared to be an inability to count little pictures in workbooks. In the workbook, there might be one picture with three little frogs, a plus sign, a picture of two monkeys in baseball uniforms, and a blank box in which you were to put the total you counted.

Our son wore glasses by this time, though he still had eye problems. We saw immediately that adding was not his problem—he became confused by the small, poorly illustrated figures jammed into the picture boxes. (Most school workbooks are appalling in literacy, content, and design.) The teacher saw it as a manifestation of her beloved theory of brain damage.

His mother saw something different—and a way to solve the problem of teaching addition. She decided to get large, familiar objects that he could handle, and this would require him not only to think but to use his whole muscle system to learn addition—and not just his eyes.

She got out several cans. She and her son got down on the kitchen floor at opposite ends. He had all the cans around him. Then she would say: "Okay, send me three cans."

Immediately, he delighted in rolling three cans across the floor to her.

Then she said, "Now send me four more cans."

He did it.

"Now, you sent me three and sent me four. Three plus four is how many?"

He saw the cans and saw the idea of it. "Seven," he said happily.

"Terrific," his mother said—because he was.

We do not offer this as a fun way to spend an afternoon with a child, but in less than a week, the boy was heavily into addition and had built a good foundation in mathematics. (Yes, he now knows all his tables, does long division with remainders, and can do fractions.)

The teacher never really believed the boy could add because she was a member of what we call the Workbook Religion. Too many teachers only believe what they see in their precious workbooks. If a child learns something in a different way, then he must not have learned it.

This dull approach to teaching is rampant in public education and is much deplored by those few educators who still believe that *all children can learn—if they are taught the right way.* And the right way for Johnny may not be the right way for Tom. Uniformity in education is strangling it.

We will mention a few really good books on education, but don't get into the trap of reading the usual claptrap the teachers are taught in education colleges.

Rosner's book is a gem. There are any number of books by Maria Montessori that express the philosophy of her approach to education, which has since grown into a worldwide movement. You can find these books in just about any library. Rosner's work in particular is a great source of ideas, especially for improving handwriting and remembering arithmetic facts. (At the back of this book is a full bibliography of the books we recommend.)

No parent should be without Rudolf Flesch's classic book—recently reissued—called *Why Johnny Can't Read— and What You Can Do About It.* It created a storm when it first appeared in 1955, and the education establishment is still down on it. It contains a fine, rational system for teaching children who have trouble in school because of widely used —and misguided—"reading systems." He has also come out with a follow-up book with updated facts and figures called *Why Johnny Still Can't Read,* but this is more an argument about the lacks in education and does not go as deeply as his first book into his system of phonics as a method for teaching reading. He is a clear writer and no parent will have any trouble following his thoughts.

While we're at it, we strongly recommend that you read the late John Holt's pioneering book, *Teach Your Own.* Holt was a schoolteacher who became disillusioned with the public system and believed that parents fed up with the things that happen to kids in schools can solve the problem by taking them out of school and teaching them at home.

It should be noted that home education is often opposed by state authorities, but parents have a legal right to prove that they can provide a better education than the state can. Some parents win this argument—with a good lawyer. Others find that they are simply never challenged. The laws, and the zeal of school boards to enforce them, vary from state to state and from district to district. In some school districts parents have been able to get approval for a home school setup from their school board—though it will often involve time-wasting consultation and test-taking provisions to be carried out with school personnel. Some people find this worthwhile just to avoid potential legal hassles.

We mentioned earlier Marva Collins, a Chicago educator. She co-authored a book called *Marva Collins' Way* (with Civia Tamarkin), which is full of anger and hope. She was tired of seeing black kids from poor ghetto neighborhoods being warehoused in education systems that conditioned them to a life of failure. She opened her own defiant school in the ghetto and it has thrived in the past fifteen years. Many of her successful students were once labeled retarded, emotionally disturbed, or learning-disabled in public or other private schools. Of them she says: "The first thing I did was toss aside all the reports and cumulative records. My experience had shown me that those reports were wrong more than they were right. I had seen too many children with their personalities ink-blotted, their IQs probed, and their every move analyzed—children written off as losers."[3] Marva Collins has had to battle a largely hostile education establishment in Chicago—but she is winning the battle.

Read these books and listen to these people because you and John Holt, Marva Collins, Jerome Rosner, and others have this in common: You all believe that children who have been short-changed in traditional education can be taught, no matter how difficult it is, with strength and love and patience.

That is what the magic feather really is. The magic feather is the need in the child to know that he cannot fail, that you—his parents—will not let him fail any more than you will let him be hurt or be afraid. A child has a right to a true education and not the phony education being peddled in the name of Special Education.

As one woman told us: "A bunch of pompous, arrogant shrinks almost had me convinced that my five-year-old son needed their help. It's taken me months to get back my confidence in myself and my son, and now I think we're going to be all right. It took me a while, but I learned to recognize bullshit when I see it."

Here is the way to teach your child out of his problem:

1. Organize your own thoughts about the problem. Once you have it straight, get ready to talk to your child.

2. Tell your child in clear language what the problem is and that you are going to work with him to remedy it. Be straight with him—tell him that you and he are going to be doing something that is difficult and involves hard work. Tell him that the difficulty and the hard work are things you know he can handle. Tell him and show him in every way that you will not let him fail.

3. Explore the ideas of others. Look around your community to see if there are teachers, tutors, librarians, or special groups that may help you achieve your goals.

4. Realize you are not alone. In a hostile world, there are quite lovely and dedicated people who want to help your Johnny almost as much as you do. There are other parents who can provide moral support. There are people in your family who will stand by you. There are good private schools left that have not swallowed the lies of the psychoeducators. Many of the tutors who may be working with children in your area may be former teachers fed up with the way the schools damage kids.

Some of the teachers you will find are YMCA coaches and music teachers, church leaders who know how to talk to your child and to you and who will support you.

5. Tackle the education problems slowly and surely.

Remember to review all you have taught. If one method is not working—and give it time—try something else.

6. A good way to check your child's progress against public school standards is to get a book called *What Did You Learn in School Today?* by Bruce and Christine Baron and Bonnie MacDonald. This book offers useful reading tests and a checklist of where each grade usually is in math or writing skills. The book is by teachers and contains the standard stuff about learning disabilities and emotional problems, but you can skip that and just use the useful parts.

7. One of the joys of teaching a child on your own is not having to follow a public school's curriculum. If Johnny picks up reading quickly, challenge him more and more with second- or third- or fourth-grade work. And if it's taking him a little longer—so what?

8. Try things that people say your child is not mature enough to do. For example, we taught our son to touch-type on a home computer at the age of nine. He can now type his classwork in fourth grade if he wants to. He loves the freedom—especially since writing is still difficult for him. He touch-types letters to his aunt and his grandma, and, in turn, this new skill has allowed him to expand his range of language. You have to believe there are all sorts of things kids can do. If elephants can fly—and they can with a magic feather—kids can become fantastic learners. All of them. All the time.

9. Knock off once in a while. Remember that forty-five minutes a day is the average time a child spends in regular school actually responding to academic tasks. The rest of the time is used up with socializing activities or paperwork routines, like calling roll or lining up to go to the art room. An hour a day of concentrated learning is an awful lot.

And learning is not just what you do when you read a book or write an essay. It is exploring the world, going to the zoo and learning where tigers come from; it is learning to shop in a grocery and make change; it is everything new in the world. And when you are a child, the world *is* new.

10. Read to your child, all the time, no matter how old he is. Read things that interest him, even if it's the same Dr. Seuss book over and over, and then gradually use the reading-aloud habit to get him interested in more books. Break off sometimes to talk about what you're reading together and to make sure he's following the story. Analyzing the story in terms of *who* the main character is, *why* he is doing something, or *what* is likely to happen next is good practice. Ask him to read to you, too.

11. Board games and card games are a good way to vary the routine, and they provide some good practice in concentrating, categorizing things, planning ahead, and reading and following directions for children who need drill in those areas.

12. The biggest secret about teaching your child on your own is how much fun it turns out to be. It is rewarding, not only to your child, but to you. You learn together. You sense again the fun of discovery. Your mind comes awake to new ideas and challenges. He will learn a lot—and so will you.

17

Making Schools Work

The public school system can be reformed. We think it will have to reform to survive.

Public school enrollment continues to decline. We are surprised by how many upper-middle-class parents have told us they never even considered sending their children to public schools. Private schools currently enroll about one-eighth of the school population, and the proportion has been growing every year.

The public schools, confronted by the evidence that fewer and fewer parents who can afford choice send their children to the free public school, try to blame the failure not on educators but on the fact that they have to "take everyone." In trendy pop sociology, there is a great deal of discussion of "the underclass," which, educators warn us, will be the main clients of the public school, unless the

upper-middle class mends its ways and agrees to sacrifice
its children to save the jobs of public school teachers.

The underclass, which is mostly black or Hispanic, is
thought to be hopeless and permanently dependent on the
benevolence and institutional generosity of the rest of us.
This bilge bubbles at the heart of not only the public system
in general but the Special Education subsystem in particular. Kids are hopeless, so teach them to live with failure.

That is what the public schools are good at. They work
their magic best with people who have no alternative but
to sit still for their experimentation and pseudoscientific
theorizing. They cannot see that in allowing the Special
Educators and psychotesters to carve empires inside of
public education, they are threatening their own legitimacy
—and their own jobs and place in the community.

Parents are increasingly horrified by the inhuman approach to education taken in too many public schools in the
country. The causes of this approach are many, the consequences are tragic.

Dr. Benjamin Spock speaks out against the increasing
competitiveness in public schools that forces out the slow
learners into slow tracks and emphasizes good grades over
good education.

> Society is much too competitive and schools are much
> too competitive. The only country that is worse off than we
> are is Japan.
>
> When I was in Japan, the educators there told me there
> is a shocking amount of suicide, even among elementary-
> school children, and it's going up. They said the reason is
> the children think they're not getting good grades. My God,
> what kind of a society makes young children want to kill
> themselves because they have not made good grades?
> Grades are not an indication of a person's worth.
>
> I condemn schools and school systems that are getting
> stricter about children having to satisfy the work in all sub-
> jects in order to get promoted to the next class. That's
> purely vindictive. Research has shown that children who are

passed anyway do better in subsequent years than children who were held back. It's strictly vindictiveness that makes us think up stricter rules to hold children back.[1]

Then Spock, in this interview, went on to say exactly what we have been trying to say: "The point of a school is not to have children measure up to a standard of the school. The school should be there to help each child, starting where he is now, to become a more mature person —not to oppress children."[2]

Sadly, public schools have fallen into traps of their own making. We would like to see reform in the public schools start by throwing out some of the traps. There is the workbook trap and the followers of the Workbook Religion who keep the trap filled with victims.

Workbooks are appalling. Have you looked at your child's workbook? They are often illiterate, usually dull, and frequently printed or illustrated poorly. In many of the publishing houses that produce such things, they are designed by people who may have had no background or experience in education. Yet teachers almost never question their directions. They follow their suggestions slavishly.

When we suggested to our son's first-grade teacher that our son would learn arithmetic better with some other approach than that represented by the workbook she was faithfully using, page by page, her eyes grew round with surprise. "But that's the way I teach arithmetic," she said. The principal, sitting in on the same conference, nodded and agreed that that settled it. The child would have to conform—the system wouldn't change.

Some children with vision problems have difficulty following the instructions in workbooks. This does not mean the child is dumb or brain-damaged or should be marched off to Special Ed classes. It means the workbooks fail to teach him.

The workbook industry is a large part of educational

publishing and, in too many cases, workbooks are routinely funneled into school systems in cozy deals made between the administrators and the textbook publishers. The teacher is then forced to build her curriculum according to the workbook.

Another reform in the public school system would be to get rid of the look-say method of teaching reading and to try phonics. Any number of new and trendy reading problems like dyslexia have increased greatly in the past thirty years simply because the method used in most schools to teach kids to read is terrible.

A lot of parents and a lot of educators have pushed, and pushed hard, for this reform in the schools, and yet little has been done. There are good reading programs, and they get results. But other reading programs remain in the schools, updated a little year by year. They teach a "controlled vocabulary" of only a few hundred words in the first two years of school. The child does not adequately learn how to sound out words for himself—though a little of what Flesch calls "phonics window dressing" is thrown in as a nod toward angry parents. Their content is empty and depressing.

Have you ever picked up your first- or second-grader's reader? Would you read such a thing for fun? Do you think your child would? Of course not. The readers are boring and demeaning. They do not have to be this way. As Siegfried Engelmann, an expert in the field, said when asked what he thought about dyslexia: "Dyslexia? I call it dysteachia." The disease is not one of learning; it is one of teaching.

The problem of teaching reading—or, rather, of not teaching reading—is ignored by too many public schools. It is a big subject, because reading is the key to learning in a complex world. To be illiterate today—and we routinely graduate illiterates from our schools—is to be permanently crippled in dealing with the rest of one's life.

We suggest again that reading by parents and educators alike the books by Rudolf Flesch on the subject—and forming a common plan of action to change our methods of teaching reading—would work wonders in our society. We have nothing to lose. The school systems could not get much worse.

Another reform—adopted in some avant-garde public systems and borrowed in theme from schools like Montessori—is breaking down uniformities. Why should all children in first grade learn just so much and no more? There is no room in the rigid classroom for a child to stretch his wings and fly.

Our son attends a school that has a lower form and an upper form. Children from roughly six to nine are in the lower form and from roughly ten to twelve in the upper form. Even this idea is stretched to include crossing from one form to the other when necessary.

A bright reader who is eight might be reading material that would be held off for fifth-graders in the public school. And if he is still working out his basic understanding of addition and subtraction, no one will throw up his or her hands in despair.

Maria Montessori believed that you could learn how to help a child learn by observing *him*. Isn't that a sensible idea? Doesn't it inspire children to believe that though they might be slow in some areas, they also might be ahead in others? Yet the public system insists there must be this grades-one-through-twelve approach to total education, with children marching in lockstep up the educational road.

Note well that when the child reaches college, however, the structure changes again. While there are some introductory courses and freshman programs, students advance in learning in various subjects at different speeds, with different goals. This is the idea behind liberal arts education; it should be the idea behind all education.

Finally, should Special Education be abolished? There is no question that a very small percentage of children need extraordinary help in achieving an education and they

should be helped out in the open, not hidden in dark closets or dummy classrooms.

We know of one case where the mother of a boy suffering from Down's syndrome insisted that the local public
school system mainstream the child in regular classes. She
had a lawyer and she used every connection to force the
system to agree with her. The system made all the usual
arguments about how other children would mock the child
for his awkward appearance. The mother was adamant.
Amazingly, the school system gave in. Over the years,
slowly and surely, the child acquired an education—a limited education, to the limits of his abilities. And over the
years, he has found more loving children than hating children. He was allowed the dignity that any human being
must have. As the mother said, "His being in the class was
as good for the class as it was for my son." Everyone
learned a capacity for patience and love.

We have a freak-show mentality in this country that
manifests itself in some of our educational abuses. We want
to hide away those who are different. More children with
special problems that have specific remedies—blind kids
who need Braille training; deaf kids who need training in
reading lips, speaking, and signing; children with physical
ailments that prevent a normal class experience—should
be helped in any way we can help them as a society.

But the point of helping people is to help them lead
normal lives. It is not to have them lead lives apart from the
rest of us. The hospital seeks to cure an ill to return a
patient back to normal—or near-normal—life. It does not
seek to keep him as a patient all his days. The blind learn
Braille—but they do not learn to be humiliated because
they are blind. The deaf learn signing—and it is a point of
pride and independence. Treat children with real handicaps with the generosity that our society believes is part of
our spirit.

In our son's school, one of the students is confined to
a wheelchair. It is remarkable to see the care the other

children show for her. They are not only engaged in the act of learning in school, but they are learning a little about love and charity and the beauty that is in all of us.

All of these suggestions strike schoolteachers as heresy and horrify defenders of the rigid system. We gave a talk one day to a teachers' group in Wisconsin and suggested that the problem of making children literate writers would be solved if every child in every grade wrote a page a day and kept it in a book to be read and corrected for grammar, from time to time, by every teacher. After twelve years of writing, the schools would not graduate any illiterates. What was the reaction of the audience of teachers to this idea? "That would be too much work for us!" is the way the leader of the protesters put it.

Why does everything have to be easier for the teacher before it is sanctified in educational practice? Whatever their salary levels—and some are extremely high, even in public school systems—public school teachers work approximately nine months a year, with generous holidays during the school year as well. We think they deserve the time off, because teaching can be an extremely tiring, emotional experience and teachers need more "recharging" of their batteries than those in less challenging jobs.

But if a teacher isn't teaching during those nine months—if he is lazy enough to let the workbook do the work for him or too uninterested to find a special approach to reading for a special boy in class—then he is stealing for a living and ought to admit it.

We have observed school systems in both England and France. In many ways, they are even worse than our own. They have institutionalized the idea of caste and class—some children will succeed because they go to the right schools and receive the correct education, others are condemned to lives of drudgery or unemployment because they have failed some test or other at some point in their school lives. In particular, the French have institutionalized the idea of Special Education to the point where a *third* of all children in French public schools are in special low-track classes.

This has cost both countries greatly. In France, again, observe that the 1968 riots in Paris and elsewhere that nearly toppled the government began as a protest against the rigidity of French education. A more middle-class revolt—but not much less violent—occurred throughout France three years ago, when the state—which funds all Catholic schools—sought to take control of the Catholic schools and introduce public curricula. The government backed down on that one, as tens of thousands of outraged parents took to the streets in protest.

Can it happen here? It is happening here today as parents and children discover the reality of public education—and march into private schools.

While public education appears to be modern, dressed up with pseudoscientific terminology to mask shoddy courses and shoddy classroom techniques, it is usually miles behind the rest of the world in ideas.

We are in a computer age and will be for some time. How many children—and especially boys—are taught to type in their twelve years of school? And yet, if you cannot type, you will not be able to communicate effectively in a new age in which every office, factory, and garage is going to be linked to computers.

We are constantly pestered by school systems to join faculty panels to explore new ways to make their Special Education system work better. After a few tries at cooperating with such panels, we have given up. *The vast majority of educators in public systems are only interested in justifying the system —not in reforming it.*

And yet reform is the only thing that will ensure the survival of public education in the next century in this country. The smoldering rage of the vast middle class against the public school system—which the middle class supports—is going to explode someday into abolishment of the public system as it could be, and it will be turned into a weak holding tank for those the society calls its under-class. The rest of the country will go the private school route.

As Dr. Cecilia Pollack wrote ten years ago: "After more than a decade of analyzing children's learning difficulties, we are forced to look to the role of the schools as an important causative factor."[3]

If teachers and administrators do not take the steps now to really shake up the public school systems, the schools will collapse. The remarkable increase in numbers and enrollments at private schools attests to this. The national media is full of stories about private schools bursting at the seams, while overfunded public systems collapse into anarchy, with failing test scores for the few too-poor or neglected students left in the public system.

18

Private Schools

Does it matter where your child goes to school? Will his future life be affected by the quality of his elementary education? Most parents wouldn't hesitate to answer those questions with a resounding *"Yes!"*

Real-estate advertisements frequently emphasize the quality of the school district in which the home-for-sale is located. Parents strive mightily to get their children in "good schools"—often sacrificing the family budget in the process.

Yet if you present the same questions to educators, the answer is widely debated and most teachers appear to answer *"No,"* when they are pinned down on the matter. In most discussions among educators about what is wrong with schools, very few ever want to speak about curriculum, school structure, or teacher training. A wide reading of educational literature gives the impression that these things—grouped under the heading of "quality of education"—do not matter.

What the literature is full of is dysfunctions in children, in their bodies and brains, and how children and their parents continue to fail the expectations of teachers and schools.

It is only fair to conclude that the vast majority of educators simply believe that education does not work and that relative success and failure in education is attributable to immutable physical qualities the student brings to school —or to his family background.

For example, when a child has trouble in a specific school situation, what will the educators tell troubled parents? They will insist it does no good to find a different school for the child—or a different course of studies or a different teacher—because whatever the problem, it originates with the child and it will follow him to any new classroom. In other words, if a child does not succeed in classroom A, it follows that he will not succeed in any other regular classroom.

This is not true. Teachers differ in their understanding, abilities, and their tolerance. Schools differ widely—as parents know, even if teachers don't.

Some shining school districts with all the latest equipment housed in air-conditioned classroom settings produce class after class of mediocre graduates. Some school districts with poor physical plants but dedicated and innovative teaching staffs produce graduation classes that go on to excel.

When we first wrote about Special Education problems, we received a surprising range of responses from educators. Here are two examples:

A Kentucky school principal said, "I think you have done a service by pointing out to parents that tests and evaluations have limited usefulness."

But a Special Education coordinator from a school

district in Mississippi said, "How dare you question the opinions of professionals who know more about children than you ever could?"

It is obvious to most parents—if not admitted by most educators—that a child with a school-based problem might have totally avoided trouble in one school and fallen into the horror world of phony psychometric testing in another. The problem haunting parents is that once your child has been in a bad public school and received a phony diagnosis of brain damage from some semipsychologist or even a mere tester—it is going to be very difficult to avoid having that label follow him into the next school. The laws governing education make it profitable and infinitely easier for a school to follow an earlier school's diagnosis.

And there is the "old boy" network at work as well: School personnel are very reluctant to question each other's judgments.

We have discovered cases in which parents moved across school-district boundaries to get their children out of poor class situations—and, in some cases, it has worked. The new school turned out to be more flexible in its approach to solving a child's school-based problems.

Other parents are unable to move. Still others find that moving to another public school exacerbates the problem —the second school does a knee-jerk reaction to the first school's diagnosis, and now two schools have voted against the child.

The alternative for many is private school. Unfortunately, there is no universal guide to private schools. They can be even more variable than public schools.

We have dipped into the subject—and barely gotten wet. But we have made a beginning and share our information, because we all have to start someplace.

We find church-related schools tend to be pretty rigid about discipline and conformity. Both the Catholic Church and various Protestant denominations have set up a large number of private schools over the years. The Catholic

Church, in particular, created a strong network of private schools in the large cities of the northeast, following the immigrant (and largely Catholic) tide moving into the country after the 1840s. Until recently, it was considered the duty of every Catholic parent to make a sacrifice to ensure that his children attended Catholic schools.

The rise of Special Education has changed this attitude, because Catholic schools—like all private schools—find it a good deal easier to turn over children with school-based problems to the dumping bins of Special Ed—and more and more do so.

Not all church-related schools, however, are cut from the same cloth. We have discovered innovative curricula, dedicated and sympathetic teachers, and a sense of mission that carries the day for any number of church schools.

Other private schools have been set up primarily to profit from the pressure parents are under to seek "therapy" for children with school-based problems. Some of these schools make an honest effort to teach children; others are old-fashioned horror factories with sadistic teachers and a prisonlike discipline system that would make good raw material for a Dickens novel.

The parent has to understand that he is the expert—even if he does not feel prepared to be an expert. There are schools that work—and it is up to parents to find them. Unfortunately, the process is not easy.

We have talked to literally hundreds of parents who have had to deal with an adverse school situation. What follows is what we have distilled from those conversations.

Children are well aware when they have been called "unfit" by a school. You can't fool children and you can't sugar-coat the unpalatable. One of the easiest ways to counteract a child's self-doubts is to get him into a school where he is accepted.

Only the most socially isolated child is going to be unaware of his "difference" from the other kids, if he is kept at home while his friends go to school.

We greatly admire the groups of parents who have succeeded in setting up home-school programs that often involve a number of families. This kind of arrangement gives the child the best of both worlds: The kind of caring, quality instruction that involved parents can give, along with a wide range of social contacts. But parents who cannot provide such a situation will be hard-pressed to solve the problem of social acceptance for a child kept out of school.

Academic standards are important—but they are not more important than children. The *D* you received in spelling in second grade is a laughable dim memory to you now —so keep grades your child receives in perspective.

A child who has been labeled a failure in one school setting does not need to fail in another. Beware of the kind of educator who speaks of separating "quality" students from "poor-quality" students. Some private schools require even preschoolers to go through a battery of psychometric tests to gain entrance to kindergarten! This procedure is harmful and useless and it speaks of a failure of the school and its curriculum.

At the other end of the scale is the kind of classroom setting where standards and goals are lowered to accommodate a child's supposed handicaps. This is the trap of Special Education—all it teaches a child is to be a failure and to be content with failure and to expect nothing but failure in life.

The goal of a good school is to help all children in it develop themselves in an atmosphere of encouragement and confidence. That is also the goal of a good teacher. All children are different; all children achieve differently; all children should be allowed to do all that they can do. The process of education is not close-ended. It continues in school, it continues at home, it continues at work and at play, it continues until the day we die.

Florence Nightingale said that the first rule of a hospital is that it do no harm to the patient. This should be the first rule of a school as well. A school should do no harm to the child.

Schools harm children every day by pinning learning-disability labels on them; by physically segregating them in special classes that aren't so special at all; by providing a high-pressure environment without tolerance for the several ways of learning. Avoid those schools, because in them your child will already start out with a negative.

A woman said to us: "Are you saying there aren't kids with reading problems? My child can't read! My child has a reading problem and I want help for him."

We answered: "Why does a child have to wear a label before you give him extra help?"

The woman thought about it for a moment and then said, "You're right. Why does he have to be labeled first?"

Ask the question of yourself and of the prospective private school. If your child needs extra help in handwriting or his reading comprehension is low, see if the school is flexible enough to work on these problems without already making the prejudgment that the child is somehow "infected" and that the school will have nothing to do with treating his disease.

Hundreds of schools have sprung up to cash in on the trend toward identifying more and more children as handicapped. Some are reasonable and can provide support to a child who needs school help. Too many, though, use unsound teaching techniques derived from crackpot educational theories based on a child's mental deficits.

Before committing your child to such a special school, examine it closely. Do the teachers consult together on individual cases, so that if one approach to learning doesn't work well, maybe another teacher has another idea? Do they have rigid ideas about what a "learning-disabled" child is or about how "emotionally disturbed" children should have their behavior modified? *Be especially cautious of behavior modification methods.* Demand to know exactly what they are, when they are used, and what is the physical result of these methods.

Finally, does the school talk you out of having high expectations for your child because of his learning disabilities? If the school has already thrown in the towel on a child before tackling his problems, it's better to skip the school altogether.

There are no hard rules for examining a private school that might be suitable for your child. The unfortunate fact is that teachers and principals may talk as though they understand and "care for every child"—the sugar-coated phrase—but then they turn out in practice to be devotees of the Special Education religion after all.

The fact is that all children with school-based problems can learn in school. There are many proven teaching techniques that work. Unfortunately, they are rarely used—particularly in the rigid hierarchy of public school systems.

The principles of good teaching apply to all children and they are simple:

1. Respect the child.

2. Show patience and a willingness to work with that child's particular problems, instead of rigidly adhering to some vague scientific theory or fixed curriculum schedule.

3. Teaching is opening up learning—and then standing back to let the learner learn. This implies a willingness to let a child work at his own pace rather than march to the insistent beat of a master schedule.

4. As the teacher respects the child, the child respects the teacher, himself, and his fellow learners. The good teacher can show what behavior is acceptable and what is not and can work with the parents and the child to make him understand.

5. The good teacher tries untiringly to find the key to trigger a child's natural eagerness to learn—and all children have this—by engaging him in his own education and making him a full partner in the process.

If those ideas sound impossible—well, they aren't. There are good teachers; there are good schools. But we all know how rare they are.

In our case, we found a small Montessori-method private school in another suburb. When we called the school, we mentioned that our son had problems in the public school—though we didn't go into the horror story of his psychological testing (don't tempt saints). We said he had eye problems and trouble writing small enough to complete workbook assignments.

The teacher said, "Oh, that's all right. He can write on unlined paper or the blackboard. We don't use workbooks here."

We were stunned and happy. It was the first sensible thing we had heard from anybody connected with education in two years. The teacher was saying what all good teachers would say: If the child has a problem, we'll devise a way to work around it.

Our son has been in Montessori-method schools ever since. He has overcome nearly all of his school problems and has turned out to be a rather bright, curious, and competent young man. Because we know about Montessori, we want to share the information. Besides the hundreds of Montessori schools, there are some public and private schools that have adopted some of the Montessori approaches to education.

Maria Montessori was the first woman to receive a medical degree in Italy, getting her papers at the University of Rome in 1894. A devout Catholic, she had a strong social-improvement urge and decided to change the way children were taught in schools then. (We note with chagrin that she was also caught up in some of the fashionable quackery of her day as well—she believed that measurement of skull capacities could determine intelligence.)

She studied how children in the slums of Rome learned from each other, and her great insight into the learning process led to her method. Her first subjects would certainly be in Special Education today. They were poor kids from orphanages in Rome, as well as from mental hospitals. They were invariably from poor backgrounds. She studied the way they learned things. She saw universals in these particulars.

Next, she turned to some tough slum kids living in a sort of public-housing complex in the Italian capital. They were the sort of children who would wear labels like "socio-culturally retarded" today or "predelinquents." The authorities considered them unteachable and did not object to Maria Montessori trying her system on them. She taught them. And they learned.

What was her secret? She was a student of the work of a French doctor named Seguin, who had developed a number of physical and sensory activities to develop mental processes in retarded children. She synthesized his ideas with her own and applied them to all children.

She believed that a child learns with his whole body— with his eyes, ears, by touching and feeling, by tasting. He learns to read with more than eyes and ears. All the senses are involved. So all the senses should be *engaged.* For instance, she made letters out of sandpaper, so that children, through touching, seeing, and understanding shapes, could learn to write before they could even learn to read.

Through these materials—still in use in Montessori schools after nearly a century—and the special year-long training required of teachers at Montessori centers throughout the world, the typical Montessori classroom is a laboratory of colors and shapes, in which children work things out by themselves, correct their own mistakes, learn through growing, and are given the freedom to experiment —and even be wrong.

The classroom setting is disciplined because the teachers (called "directors") guide the children firmly to learn to respect themselves, others, the work they are doing, and the whole community of the classroom.

Invariably, regular educators hate Montessori schools.

The fact that most of them have never observed a Montessori classroom—and they invite observations from parents and outsiders—doesn't stop the hatred. One psychologist told us that he knew Montessori schooling was a terrible method because "in those schools, the children just run around." Absolutely wrong—but why bother to correct people who don't want to get their facts straight?

Discipline in Montessori schools is flexible and constant. It is like the restraints we impose on ourselves instinctively in adult society; it is what makes civilization civil. Maria Montessori said children reduced to immobility in an ordinary classroom are hurt. "They are not disciplined; they are annihilated."

Our son was turned off early by the "Look at the cute bunny rabbit" method of teaching in his first school experiences. Too many bad teachers in too many early grades try to trick children into thinking the work they are doing is really only a matter of playing games.

Dr. Bruno Bettelheim, the world-famous child psychiatrist, noted in a book he wrote with Karen Zelan that this strain of pseudoteaching runs throughout education, particularly in textbooks and workbooks. He calls it "the fun morality" and says that it harms the education of a child.

Montessori schools do not indulge in "the fun morality." The structure in the classroom is to let children learn to do work—the work of learning. They teach order by example and direction. Our very typical ten-year-old boy actually makes his bed every morning and cleans his own room once a week!

The method does not use rewards or punishments to guide children. Maria Montessori thought children should be respected too much to be insulted with cheap rewards.

Over the years, some Montessori ideas have begun to filter into regular classrooms here and there. Be on the lookout for them.

1. Children, Montessori believed, have sensitive periods when they are able to learn things more easily than

during other periods. That's why children are taught to write before they learn to read, because a child is very interested in the feel and shape of things—like those sandpaper letters—before realizing what wonderful things you can do with letters.

2. Classrooms are vaguely ungraded, so that a range of children in different age groups can come together to learn at different speeds. Older children learn to help younger children—thus learning something themselves—and younger children are encouraged to imitate the role model of the older children; just as it works in large families!

3. Each child learns differently, at different speeds, in different times. Give each child his own time.

Our son has been in Montessori schools for three years. He is teaching himself and learning with others. He is an instructor—teaching those younger—and a learner. He never wants to miss a day of school. He brings home acres of writing—essays, descriptions, diaries of daily events. He . . . but then, we are now falling into the stage of an adult conversation when grown-ups start pulling out their children's baby pictures and bragging about their kids.

A note of warning about Montessori schools: Most end with kindergarten, a few go through eighth grade. As our neighbor John, who has a son in our son's class, noted, "Montessori schools are too positive and encouraging to children. They don't prepare kids to face reality."

He went on: "Montessori ends with sixth grade. Sooner or later, every child is going to have to come up against the *real* schools and find out all this stuff about cooperation and concern for each other and respect is out the window. They are going to have to go cold turkey."

There are many other private schools, of course. Noted before, the Roman Catholic Church runs the largest private school system in the country. Church schools are booming. Generally, tuition costs are much lower than they are at other private schools because taxes are less, salaries are ridiculously low compared with salaries of public school teachers, and there are certain subsidies from within the Church itself to maintain some marginal schools.

It was a tenet of American Catholicism for most of a century that Catholic parents were obliged to send their kids to Catholic schools. As noted in our story—and in other case histories we have received—this sense of obligation is breaking down quickly. Catholic parents are refusing to send their kids to Catholic schools; some Catholic schools are refusing to take in "problem" children, even if they are Catholic, preferring to dump their problems on the public school system.

Public school officials know this. They make a loud point about the practice of private schools to select only "the best and brightest" for their classrooms and to send the also-rans to public schools, thereby depressing public test and reading scores.

There is truth to this. There is also a lot of hot air in it. The private schools are booming and the sheer numbers of kids in private schools today indicates that elitism is not the only factor at work. There is a quiet revolution going on. For fifteen years, the shifts in educational preferences among parents—particularly the American middle class—toward private school education has been noted but not really talked about. Forests have been chopped down to provide newspapers with space to talk about the crises in public education and the failures of public schools and the wild new theories to be applied in Special Education to facilitate learning—even while learning declines.

But who is talking about private schools? Millions of American parents are making sacrifices to send their children to someplace that is not a public school. It happens in the ghetto and the barrio, in the villages with wide lawns and narrow minds, in cities and in the countryside. It is a grass-roots movement—and the education establishment would like to pretend it is not there.

Our society has changed. Schools have become more than places of learning. The American family drifts apart slowly in the era of the two-income household, and schools become a child's second home, complete with after-school child-watching services. They were never intended to serve this function—but the function is needed and the demand for it soars.

Schools have become the focus of integration efforts in the North, particularly in large cities. Methods are often crudely enforced to break up apparent patterns of segregation that only ensure more segregation in the years to come. School busing for integration has been criticized even by black leaders like the Reverend Jesse L. Jackson— yet it continues.

We have found cases where children as young as six are bused two and three hours a day to satisfy a court-ordered program of integration. We are not ready to take on the subject of school busing for integration—that's another book and a half—but it is no secret that parents with the means and will power (black and white) will opt for the easy retreat to private schools, rather than have their kids become unwilling school commuters.

In a sense, people in very small towns and rural areas have a better chance at a better education simply because of the lack of choice. If there is only the public school in town and no other option, then the public school is made to work for children.

Large cities are the traditional American gateways of the poor emerging to a better life. Public schools were once passports to that better life. (The history of the New York public school system and its love affair with immigrants is the stuff of a romantic novel—and hundreds have been written in that context!)

But once the vocal, concerned, and informed part of the electorate elects to abandon the public school system because it is easier to run from problems than to fight them, the public schools have lost the war for viability.

The Reagan administration and any number of politicians of both parties have campaigned for a voucher system or some sort of tax break for parents who send their kids to private schools. The idea isn't new. It was proposed in the Kennedy administration a generation ago. But it takes on a sense of urgency today, as parents continue to opt out of what they perceive as a crumbling, inhuman education system. And you'd have to be blind not to realize that the horror they perceive in part is the jungle growth of Special Education in the public schools. No one wants to wear labels. No one wants their kids to wear labels.

Rather than waste so much research on why public schools fail, why don't the researchers try to study private schools—and why they work?

Marva Collins has campaigned for this approach from her West Side Prep school in Chicago for fifteen years. It is a school in a ghetto and it teaches children of the ghetto —although its success has attracted children of people definitely not on the downscale (including the son of a former Chicago police chief).

Marva Collins has been publicly challenged during those years by the educational establishment to "prove" her methods work. Why should she take the time to prove something that is obvious to the thousands of parents—and children—who have scraped up hard-earned tuition money over the years to send their kids to her school?

Or take the case of all-black Holy Angels school, located on the South Side of Chicago in the heart of what the U.S. census has labeled the most impoverished area in the metropolis. As noted in national publications such as *Time* magazine, Holy Angels works. Catholic and non-Catholic parents send their kids to this little Catholic school, where strict discipline and intensely devoted instructors have combined to create class after class of children who consistently score way ahead of their public school counterparts.

The old arguments about selecting the "best and brightest" don't work here. These kids are the same as their peers in the crumbling Kenwood neighborhood slum. The school and parish are poor. Why does it work? No one wants to know.

The secrets are too easily discovered. The good schools have them: love, intent, hard work, a flexible approach to teaching, dedication, commitment. Those words explain seeming miracles.

But the public school systems remain defensive bullies, sulking in the corner of education, offering excuses to explain away a system that doesn't work. We have too many black kids, and black kids from the ghetto don't want to learn, they say. And then you point out a Holy Angels or West Side Prep and the argument explodes.

Too many children are brain-damaged or disturbed or retarded, whine the public schools, and there's nothing we can do with them. Yet there are all sorts of private tutors, private schools that prove children with learning problems can be taught to overcome them without being labeled and without the rigmarole of Special Ed segregation.

We are not championing the cause of private education, voucher systems, or tax credits. We report on what we see and what is common knowledge. Because private schools exist in numbers, and are growing and thriving at a time when public education is in decline, they are obviously the alternative that millions have chosen.

We think that the whole Special Education movement is a giant hoax designed to breathe billions of dollars and temporary life into the corpse of public education. It is a shameful misuse of public monies and a tragic misuse of the lives of children.

When public education grows up and accepts the responsibility for teaching all kids, public education will become healthy again. Until then, there are young lives waiting. And the private schools—the whole crazy quilt of alternative education—may be what they are waiting for now.

19

Seeing and
Hearing

Teachers and parents who have read this book, and agreed with much of what we have shown, still might have this reservation: While it is true that schools are too rigid and that psychometric tests are wildly inaccurate, isn't it also true that there are children who are simply "different"? And if there are, isn't it important to find out how and why these children are different and what can be done about their problems?

We want to answer fully and carefully. Who are the different ones? Learning-disability theorists who have been trying to isolate and describe different children for so long, think they make up 2 or, at most, 3 percent of the learning population. No one disputes that they are usually boys. They have difficulties with language and motor coordination and lag behind the "average" children—though the average can vary from class to class and from school to school. They have troubles, on the whole, but the troubles do diminish with age and in some cases disappear entirely in time without treatment.

The different ones are not necessarily inferior. They sometimes have a great deal to offer. A child with difficulties in language often shows a startling ability in another area—music or mathematics in particular.

Harvard psychologist Norman Geschwind, who has made a study of different children, goes so far as to say that if their problem could be seen as pathology, it was "a pathology of superiority as well as inferiority."[1]

In too many schools, a different child is quickly labeled as learning-disabled. In other schools, he is labeled emotionally disturbed. In another spectrum of schools, he is tagged retarded. The important thing seems to be the label. The difference in labeling procedures is quite arbitrary.

We have tried to say in different ways, over and over, that labeling children does them no good. Worse, it does them harm from the beginning. *The label itself is a negative thing.* Helping a child overcome a particular learning problem does not mean he has problems in all other areas and does not mean he has no areas of superiority, either. Why can't teachers simply help kids without labeling them? Why are labels so important?

We think it is clear that most of these children suffer mainly from a failure to develop their language skills as well as the "average" child. A child's main task before he goes to school is to learn how to use language to communicate. It is a tremendously complicated thing to learn. He needs not only to understand a range of vocabulary, but to comprehend the way speech is put together to form sentences and to learn how to listen to these sentences in such a way that their elements and their meanings are fully understood. He further must be able to do this with such ease that the understanding is almost automatic.

People talk quickly. The child must catch the words and respond. Teachers talk to groups of children; the child must understand that the directions relate to him and must be followed in sequence, as though the teacher were speaking only to him. He must learn to understand what is to be done, to translate it into action, and to do this fairly quickly.

He must be able to talk. He must know what words are "appropriate" (using the educator's stiff-lipped term) and what words are socially acceptable.

He must understand how to imitate the normal rate and pitch of speech. He must not talk too much and he must not talk too little.

He must learn not to confuse pronouns or place names. He must learn a sense of time in speech—talk of those things that happened yesterday and will happen tomorrow. If he does any of these things badly, he will confuse teachers, frighten them, and slate himself for psychotesting. That is the truth of it. The pressure is put on from the first day of school. It is a crying shame.

Despite these tasks, most children do them well enough. So why do some six-year-olds lag in language development? And why are so many of them boys?

In truth, boys learn differently from girls. Nobody who has really studied the literature on learning disabilities can fail to notice this overwhelming fact. It is obviously discriminatory against males to expect them to meet early standards of language development set as an "average" that includes females in the same age group. It is obvious that in language development, in the early grades boys as a group rate far below girls. They catch up in time, by their teens, but by then damage can be done to them by labeling in Special Education.

Many children—and this is a vague field full of too many guesstimates—have problems with perception, with seeing and hearing, that manifest themselves in school as language-development problems. Why language? Because that is where school places the emphasis. If a child is slow to speak at home, he has few problems with that lack because less language is demanded of him in the home setting.

We are saying that children who experience difficulties, for any reason, in seeing or hearing—or in interpreting what they see and hear—will spend a great deal of their energy in preschool years trying to make sense out of the world around them. In practical effect, this means they have less energy left over for practicing their language skills to the point of fluency demanded by most schools at age six.

There is persuasive evidence that the problems of seeing and hearing—simple, physical problems—lie at the root of the trouble for many (even most) of the small percentage of kids who are "different."

For forty years, people who work in child vision development have known that children whose eyes, for whatever reason, do not work well together have slower language development. They know also that such children can exhibit the signs that so distress teachers—they don't understand the significance of left and right, their hand preference is a variable, their eye-hand coordination is imprecise, and they confuse letters like *b* and *d* (and show other symptoms of what some continue to call dyslexia).

Still other researchers who work on the way children learn to sound out words know that children who fail to break words down into sounds adequately have great difficulty with phonetics. The children pass the standard hearing test that school nurses give, but they have not learned adequately how to listen to speech.

Training programs that drill these children on sounds and sequences in speech have been shown to have overwhelming success in overcome reading difficulties—yet most schools persist in requiring a more complex "looksay" method of reading that has nothing to do with phonetics and insist that if the basic hearing test is passed, nothing can be wrong with the way a child hears.

What should be done with such "different" children?

There are only two schools of thought on this: (1.) They should be sent to psychotesters to find out whether they're retarded, brain-damaged, or crazy, and they should be so labeled and dumped in Special Education bins; and (2.) They should be taught to develop the skills they lack, regardless of labels. Choose one.

At this point, some parents might think the problem could not be as simple as seeing and hearing. There are many more children labeled learning-disabled now than there were a generation ago. Where did all these defective children come from?

There are two reasons for the increase in "different" children. First, schools—particularly tax-supported schools—have been under increasing pressure in the past decade to show what they are doing to teach kids. Parents are dissatisfied with falling test scores and increasing numbers of illiterate graduates. To justify the record of failure in public schools, more "different" kids must be uncovered and labeled to show the problem is not of the schools' making—but of the defective children themselves. In other words, if we have 2 or 3 percent of the school population who are different—but whose problems can be resolved—then there is no justification for the vast Special Ed bureaucracy.

The second reason, we have come to conclude, is that television is part of the problem—but in an unexpected way. Talk to teachers as we have, and you get the idea that they have *overestimated* young children's conceptual abilities. This generation of children, raised on television, presents an impression of verbal sophistication that masks the fact that they are still children. Teachers too often imagine —because of a child's rotelike verbal skill in repeating the phrases he picks up from a daily dose of TV watching—that they are dealing not with children but with tiny adults. These tiny adults can talk the automatic slang of cops and tough guys, but they are really still undeveloped minds who have not had time to form basic concepts. Kids today talk a good game but they are probably no more sophisticated than children of a generation ago.

Thus, the teacher in our son's public school first grade assigned her class a copying exercise about the dangers of nuclear waste. What possible relevance could that have to a six-year-old? Nuclear waste? It wasn't important to inquire if anyone even understood the term. Yet it seemed reasonable to the teacher because these children could repeat pseudosophisticated dialogue picked up from watching "The A-Team" or "Hill Street Blues."

Children who catch on to language early have at least three years in front of a television set to hone their skills. But what about children who are not allowed to watch a lot of junk TV? Or children who—because of visual or hearing problems—are using those first five years to make sense of the world around them and are neglecting their language-development skills? These children all go to school together and are suddenly shocked to find how different they are from the other children.

One teacher who spoke to us of the changes in children she has taught over thirty years in kindergarten said, "These days, we just pick up where 'Sesame Street' leaves off."

A generation ago, schools gave children practice in rule following, small-motor coordination, recitation as an aid to language—but now these procedures are usually ignored. And the child who needs that practice loses out because the schools assume a level of sophistication in children commensurate with their language skills.

Not every school problem can be solved by improving a child's hearing and his vision. But no one has offered any proof yet of how widespread these problems are; and we think our guess—based on interviews, reading the literature on the subject, and consulting with teachers and parents—is as good as anyone else's in the field. We think vision and hearing problems lie at the core of a majority of the kids labeled different.

We think vision and hearing problems are routinely overlooked by schools—and even by anxious parents. We think that all children—and all adults as well—have problems from time to time with some aspect of work or development. It is the clear duty of parents to look at these problems in development as problems requiring specific solutions—and to stop looking for some mysterious underlying mental disease that probably does not exist.

Every parent whose child seems to show some difficulty with language—and that can range from a child who acts deaf at times to what some schools call "hyperactivity" —should seriously question whether the child has learned to use his eyes and ears properly. As a first step, we recommend that parents look for help in Jerome Rosner's tests and teaching systems for visual and auditory perception described in his fine book, *Helping Children Overcome Learning Difficulties.*

Our son's eyes crossed visibly at the age of five. We thought this must be causing him stress. We believed it must be at the base of his coordination problems—his failure to "color in the lines."

We consulted experts. They patronized us. They assured us that vision had nothing to do with his ability to write, to speak, to draw.

We went to our pediatrician. We were directed to a well-recommended ophthalmologist with an enormous practice at one of the leading university hospitals. She prescribed glasses. She said that if the glasses didn't work, she would recommend surgery.

The glasses did not help our son very much. But he worked hard despite what we thought was still a vision problem. He relied on his other faculties to help him keep up. He learned to read because he wanted to learn to read.

We questioned the ophthalmologist several times about there being another sort of vision problem. The doctor became impatient with us. We were parents; therefore, we didn't know what we were talking about.

By chance, one day, out of the blue, we received a letter from an optometrist who said he had read about our education struggle with the schools and thought our son had a binocular vision problem—his eyes didn't work together—and that he could correct it. We were skeptical. But we tried him nonetheless. He performed a simple test on our child. After the test—which caused no pain or anxiety—he said it was clear that our son was constantly switching from one eye to the other, destroying his reading comprehension and his concentration. He said a series of visual training exercises two or three days a week—for an hour at a time—spread over three months, could teach him to use his eyes more efficiently. The treatment required no drugs and no pain. We let him try. It worked.

All right. That's one story. But we have received dozens of other case histories that speak of similar experiences by parents who finally stumble upon a developmental optometrist.

Here is Jeffrey's tale. Jeffrey was a normal, healthy child who had difficulties with language, following hospitalization for a severe reaction to a measles vaccine. Fortunately for Jeffrey, his public school was not on the Special Ed bandwagon. His parents were told that Jeffrey was a slow learner and that they could not expect much from him in his school years. Everyone at school liked Jeffrey well enough—they just concluded that he was slow. When his parents asked why Jeffrey was not learning to read at grade level, one snappish teacher said the parents were pushing the boy too hard. Jeffrey's mother said solving his problems was a matter of chance:

> When it came time to take Jeffrey for his annual eye exam, I got lazy and did not make an appointment for him with the ophthalmologist we had seen in the past. Instead, we went to the optometrist at the local discount eyeglass store.
> This optometrist was fresh out of school. And he said, as previous examiners had, that Jeffrey had 20/20 vision.

But his eyes never focused together, the optometrist said, and as a result, his actual vision was usually a blur.

The guy doing the exam was having a ball. Here was something he had studied in school, and here was a kid who exemplified what he had studied.

At first I took what he said with a large grain of salt. I had heard of "lazy eye" and of crossed eyes which needed surgery, but the treatment he suggested—and the obvious relish with which he suggested it—made me worry that I had run into a real quack.

He told me Jeffrey needed special bifocal lenses to force his eyes to focus and an extensive series of visits to work on eye exercises.

But since this was the first person who had a reasonable theory of why her bright little boy was having trouble in school, Jeffrey's mother put him through a series of eye-exercise programs. In eight weeks he was reading fluently. And other things were working better for Jeffrey in school as well.

"I still don't know how, but at the same time, his speech fluency improved dramatically," his mother said. "This child, who previously used only five pronouns, suddenly understood all the pronouns and began to use tenses properly. For the first time, his verbs began to agree with his subjects."

It didn't matter at first at school. He had been put in the lowest reading group—and as a recent report on the teaching of reading puts it: "Once a bluebird, always a bluebird."[2] His group in fourth grade was a full school year behind the other kids.

Jeffrey showed pluck. He became angry and determined. The easygoing child liked so much by staff at school was not going to allow himself to be softballed into being a failure. He talked to his teacher and convinced her to allow him to take a test to get into a higher reading group. The teacher told Jeffrey's parents that Jeffrey could not possibly pass the test. He passed.

"Jeffrey is presently a high school freshman," his mother exulted. "He is successful, taking all class honors —but he still does not see himself as a very bright person. He had too many people make him believe when he was young that if anything, he was overachieving for what the teachers saw as his basic subpar abilities.

"This is not a story about Special Education," she went on to tell us. "But I think it is similar. Early on, teachers refused to accept parents' assessment of a child. They reacted to the child not as I believe a professional should —in light of his actual learning performance in the class-room—but rather as a baby-sitter would, in light of his ability to fit into the classroom structure."

Jeffrey's story is common. So is ours. We have received many histories from people who learned that their son's difficulties in school stemmed from a vision problem that could be remediated. By the time it was discovered, how-ever, in many cases it was too late; the child had been programmed to failure.

Schools rarely refer children to optometrists. Their idea of vision is static: The eye is like a camera. Their only suggestion regarding vision is the standard vision test. The standard test is based on the Snellen letter chart we have all used in school or in the eye doctor's office. It tells you about visual acuity. *Unfortunately, we have discovered that many children who have reading problems caused by vision problems turn out to have perfect visual acuity.*

Here's an oddity: Some studies show that nearsighted children do better in school than children with perfect acu-ity. Optometrists believe that nearsightedness may be an adaptation—a successful one—that children make in order to do the very close work they are required to do in schools.

The Snellen chart does not tell you how the child is using his eyes. Is he focusing them properly? Are both eyes working together? Is he having to expend so much energy just seeing the words he is trying to read that he has none left over to consider their meaning?

There is a group called developmental optometrists, who specialize in correcting vision problems of the sort described. (For names and numbers, see page 230.)

A number of vision-care professionals, particularly ophthalmologists, do not believe in vision training at all. They insist the visual system must be looked at in different terms. This debate in the vision-care establishment has been going on for decades and shows no sign of being resolved anytime soon.

We only repeat that we have been overwhelmed by the number of letters we have had from parents who have found a solution to their children's school-based problems through optometric help.

Ralph Nader, the consumer advocate, told an audience of optometrists in 1980 about the dispute and the effect it has on parents and children:

> So many children and their parents don't know why their children aren't learning, and they have all kinds of theories of course, including the temperature of the school, but certainly the visual health of the student has been shown repeatedly, in case after case, to be extraordinarily critical. . . .
>
> Which raises a broader problem: Who is right here? You talk to ophthalmologists and they say, "Forget about it, you can't exercise the eyes and deal with strabismus and so on and so forth. You know that's just a lot of quackery." And then you talk to optometrists who are very distinguished in their field and they say the ophthalmologists don't know what they're talking about and they'd better stay in their area. In the meantime, what is the consumer supposed to believe, particularly since the ophthalmologist has an M.D. after his or her name and the AMA behind him?[3]

The dispute began more than forty years ago. It really started with discoveries of an optometrist named A. M. Skeffington, who began to publicize the idea of vision as a learned skill. Skeffington began practice in the 1920s, when optometrists were sort of an adjunct to the jewelry counter in the local drugstore—they helped people pick out frames for glasses and figure out which lenses did the most for their eyes.

Skeffington made the same discovery as Maria Montessori—that vision is intertwined with the whole motor and intellectual development of the child. "The process by which man sees and gets meaning out of the world is learned," Skeffington said. "Man must learn to see."[4]

And what is learned, the optometrist reasoned, could be taught. Together with other optometrists and such child-development experts as Arnold Gesell, Skeffington began to work out the techniques that have led to vision training.

Educators frequently shoot down the idea that vision training might solve the problems that lie behind a wide range of school behavior they prefer to attribute to brain damage or emotional disturbance. *To admit that the problem might be correctable would be to admit that such children might really belong in the regular classroom.*

Dr. Richard S. Kavner, an optometrist, writes in *Your Child's Vision* that

> As a child's binocular system develops, it helps him to orient himself in space.
>
> Visual information is then interpreted along with body signals in order to properly orient the person to his world.
>
> One of the unfortunate effects of strabismus [crossed eyes] is that it interferes with this integration. It affects the child's perception of reality and as a result has a negative effect on his reality testing—his constant exploring in order to develop a stable sense of who he is.[5]

This is worth rereading. It raises a profound idea that might explain why thousands of Johnnys and Jennifers act the way they do in a school setting. They have no sense of where they are in relationship to their world.

Kavner goes on: "When the child has a turned eye, he finds he is looking in two different directions at the same time. One eye is attending to something he wants to see; the other eye is giving him information about something he has no interest in. It can be very confusing. It can look to him as if one person is sitting on top of another person. Or instead, he may see two objects that appear to be attached, although he knows this cannot be true."[6]

The causes of crossed eyes and other vision problems are many and may never be fully known. But the agonizing about the causes is irrelevant if treatment is at hand. *The problem can be corrected*—that's the important thing.

The vision training varies. Some of it can involve physical exercises like jumping on a trampoline while playing catch with the therapist. Almost all training involves writing on a blackboard, learning to copy patterns and shapes and to draw circles with both hands at the same time. In all of it, the eyes are "taught" to work together efficiently.

Some educators who know little about this subject pooh-pooh the ideas behind it and say that vision training has something to do with strengthening eye muscles. This is nonsense—it has nothing to do with strengthening muscles. It has to do with making the eyes work together to produce a single vision and to let the child see his place in the universe around him.

Look at it from a child's viewpoint: If you have been seeing double or having blurred vision since before you began school, you are unlikely to be able to correct the problem yourself. You simply do not understand how things really look to other people around you. You are aware that something is wrong—but you can't understand what the problem is. And when people let you know that you are slow, retarded, a loser—then maybe you begin to believe them.

At least one study of schoolchildren who received vision training found that common problems with reading and speech showed definite improvement. In particular, children who had problems with letter reversals—reading *b* for *d,* and so forth, the major symptoms of dyslexia and minimal brain damage in many schools—had those symptoms disappear after vision training. It seems that directionality and hand preference also are learned along with the development of vision.

Once the vision problem is corrected, it can be too late. Like Jeffrey, the child may have already been categorized in the slow group. He is certainly far behind his classmates on a number of projects. Parents of children like this should realize that once the vision problem is fixed, an intensive program of catching up academically for the child who can suddenly see is still needed.

No, we do not believe every child in Special Education today has a vision or hearing problem. But we think a lot of them do. And we think it is wrongheaded for teachers and other educators not to explore this idea of a simple physical problem holding a child back in school.

We have consulted with optometrists and read the literature and have put together a list of symptoms that might indicate your child has a vision problem. Here are signs to look for in your child that might indicate vision problems that could respond to visual training:

1. Does the child move his head when reading instead of his eyes—or does he cock his head in an awkward posture, as though looking at the page sideways?

2. Does he use his finger to trace lines in a book?

3. Does he leave out words when he reads out loud, skip lines, or seem to ignore punctuation marks?

4. Does he have trouble catching balls? Not necessarily in throwing balls, but in catching them?

5. Does he have a short attention span? Does he show stress and fatigue when reading? Does he count the pages in a book before he begins reading and try to stick to short pieces?

6. Does he read well but have difficulty remembering what he has read?

These symptoms can point to signs of visual coordination problems that can be corrected. A child should be tested thoroughly by a developmental optometrist using all his equipment in his office. But there is a simple home test that might give you a clue as to whether or not you need to pursue the matter further. It was given to us by Dr. Nast.

Roll up a piece of typing paper into a tube about eleven inches long. Have the child hold the tube up to one eye—it doesn't matter which. Stand in front of the child and hold up the palm of your hand about one inch beyond the end of the tube, with the tube focused on the palm of your hand. Your child should stare at your hand with *both eyes* and describe what he sees.

What a person with normal vision coordination sees is a hand with a circle in the middle of the palm. A person whose eyes are not working together will see the circle and the hand separately—the circle will not be in the center of the hand, and the two images may not even touch.

The test is simple, the idea behind it is complex. In normal vision, both eyes merge visual phenomena into a single image. In children whose eyes don't work together, they are getting two visions and the mind is receiving two images. Obviously, such a test might give you the clue you need to find the way to solve your child's vision problems.

To find a developmental optometrist in your area, you can consult two organizations that keep lists of them:

The Optometric Extension Program
2912 S. Daimler
Santa Ana, CA 92705

The College of Optometrists in Vision Development
P.O. Box 285
Chula Vista, CA 92012

What we have tried to emphasize in this chapter and throughout this book is that children are the responsibilities of their parents and that parents are sometimes going to have to go an extra mile or three to help their child grow in learning. A parent should look for obvious causes of childhood learning problems rather than accepting the "no-fault" theory behind everyone parroting a line about neurological damage that can't be fixed and can't be blamed on anyone.

20

Great
Expectations

School can be a frightening and Dickensian world of child
abuse. It can also be an experience leading to great expectations.

Unfortunately, abuse of children in Special Education
—because of the very nature of Special Education practiced
today in most parts of the country and in most school
systems—is growing.

We have tried to do five things in this parent's guide
to avoiding the traps of Special Education:

1. We have told you our own experiences to establish
our interest in the subject, our credentials, and why we
have pursued this subject on behalf of others. We are all in
this together.

2. We have tried to tell you in simple terms, using

layman's language, where Special Education came from and how it is based on various gimcrack theories, fraudulent research, racist attitudes long embedded into the fabric of our society (remember Goddard's ladies rejecting people as subnormal at Ellis Island because they looked "different"?). We realize that the lure of "no-fault parenting"—it is the siren song of Special Education—is powerful. Special Education tells you the child is broken and it was not your fault and let us put him away in a corner and teach him to live with his brokenness. This is morally wrong and parents who accept this nonsense are as guilty as the educators who perpetuate it.

3. We have tried to show you that you are not alone in your skepticism of what passes for Special Education. We have recounted some other experiences shared by others who have struggled against Special Education traps to show you that there are others like you, struggling like you, to save their children.

4. We have offered some advice in some areas about what is wrong with public schools, Special Education, some private schools—and what is right about different approaches to learning. We have emphasized the idea that visual problems (not merely seeing problems) may be behind a lot of school problems in kids who are otherwise bright and happy and normal. School problems are school problems—not necessarily learning problems. A child learns all the time, in all environments, from many teachers.

5. We have tried to show that you, the parent, are the primary teacher. No one is going to save your child but you —though you will be surprised by all the help you will have along the way. There are still a lot of good-hearted, commonsensical people in the world who see things clearly and speak plainly about problems like this.

If we have succeeded in any part of these goals, we are happy. Perhaps it was a good thing that all those bad things happened to us and to our son. Perhaps it can help others achieve a sense of purpose to help their own kids overcome a sad and corrupt system of noneducation called Special Ed.

Perhaps, too, we have touched the heads or hearts of a few psychologists, doctors, teachers, administrators, and principals—not to mention truly dedicated Special Education teachers—to reexamine their approaches to the problems of learning. Children are not square pegs to be fitted into round holes. Children are not computers, machines, statistical theories, bell curves, so many boxes fitting inside of so many other boxes. Children are not to be abused with words, with the vision of a future of failure, with physical methods that surpass in sheer sadism the way we treat the average convict in a penitentiary. Children are not guilty from the beginning, and to predict a future of failure for a child of four or five is a criminal, antihuman act.

We end this book with hope, because hope is what this country believes in best. We hope things are going to change from now on because of the increasing number of voices raised to protest a monstrous system of calculated inhumanity that has destroyed part of a generation of children in the schools.

In this book, we have quoted political liberals and political conservatives who agree on a common problem. We have gone to consumer activists like Ralph Nader and brave educators like Marva Collins and to clear-eyed psychiatrists like Dr. Theodore Szasz for their words and their perspectives. Not every person we quoted in this book will agree with everything we have said. No one has the whole answer. But we think we have pretty well shown that Special Education in public schools today is worse than no answer at all, and that change has to come quickly before more children are wasted.

If this book has helped you, let us know. We still have all those thousands of letters we received over the years from the time we first told our story. Let us finish with one more story.

The other day, our son took a book down from our shelves. We have a wall or two of books. He loves books and loves to read now, but this book was quite different from the usual books he reads at home and in school. This was one of Daddy's books, part of a set acquired a long time ago. He opened the book and smoothed the pages and turned to the first page. He read the title slowly: *"Great Expectations."* He looked at his mother. "What does that mean?"

"It means great things to come. It's about a boy called Pip. Remember that movie we saw? It's about Pip and about how he grows up with great expectations for his future."

"I like that movie."

"That's the book they took the movie from," his mother said.

And he nodded and said nothing more. And that night, he took the book to bed with him. And he slept with the book next to him.

Notes

Introduction

1. *The School-Age Handicapped,* Contractor Report, National Center for Education Statistics, Child Trends Inc., prepared for U.S. Department of Education (Washington, 1985), 67.

3 Testing Alec

1. Glenn Doman, *What to Do About Your Brain-Injured Child* (Garden City: Doubleday & Company, 1974), 206.

5 Aftermath of a Nightmare

1. Jean Latz Griffin, "State Suspicious of 'Handicapped' Label on Students," *Chicago Tribune,* 7 October 1984, sec. 2.

6 The Silver Lining

1. See Thomas J. Cottle, *Barred from School* (Washington: New Republic Book Company, 1976), 5.

2. Ibid., 4.

3. William H. Wilken and John J. Callahan, "Declining Enrollment: The Cloud and Its Silver Lining," in *Declining Enrollment: The Challenge of the Coming Decade*, ed. Susan Abramowitz and Stuart Rosenfeld, National Institute of Education (Washington, March 1978), 142–57.

4. Ibid.

5. Department of Education figures. See *The School-Age Handicapped*, Contractor Report, National Center for Education Statistics, Child Trends Inc., prepared for U.S. Dept. of Education (Washington, D.C.: GPO, 1985), 61; also *Exectutive Summary, Sixth Annual Report to Congress on the Implementation of Public Law 94–142: The Education for All Handicapped Children Act*, U.S. Department of Education, 1984.

6. Reported in "Disabilities in U.S. Babies Found to Have Doubled in 25 Years," *International Herald-Tribune*, 21 July 1983.

7. Larry Maheady, Bob Algozzine, and James Ysseldyke, "Minorities in Special Education," *The Education Digest* 51 (December 1985):50.

7 Where Intelligence Came From

1. Alfred Binet and Th. Simon, *The Development of Intelligence in Children*, translated from articles in L'Annee Psychologique from 1905, 1908, and 1911 by Elizabeth S. Kite (Baltimore: Williams and Wilkins, 1916), 40. Quoted in Stephen Jay Gould, *The Mismeasure of Man* (New York: W.W. Norton & Company, 1981), 151.

2. Ibid., 151–52.

3. Ibid.

4. Lewis M. Terman, *The Intelligence of School Children* (Boston: Houghton Mifflin, 1919), 288.

5. Lewis M. Terman, "The Great Conspiracy," reprinted in *The I.Q. Controversy*, ed. N. J. Block and Gerald Dworkin (New York: Random House, 1976), 35.

6. Dr. Doris Johnson, Dr. Lyndel Bullock, Dr. Laura Jordan, Howard Atlas, and Dr. Cindy Terry, *LD or Not?*, Illinois State Board of Education pamphlet, July 1984.

8 Emotions

1. *The School-Age Handicapped*, Contractor Report, National Center for Education Statistics, Child Trends Inc., prepared for

U.S. Dept. of Education (Washington, D.C.: GPO, 1985), 61.

2. Daniel P. Hallahan and James M. Kaufman, *Exceptional Children: Introduction to Special Education* (Englewood Cliffs, N.J.: Prentice-Hall, 1982), 158.

3. Thomas S. Szasz, M.D., *The Manufacture of Madness* (New York: Harper & Row, 1970), 35.

4. Ibid., 35.

5. Ibid., 283.

6. James E. Ysseldyke, Ph.D., "Current Practices in Making Psychoeducational Decisions About Learning Disabled Students," *Journal of Learning Disabilities* 16 (April 1983):228.

7. Laurence Lieberman, "On Aggressiveness," *Journal of Learning Disabilities* 16 (January 1983):64.

8. Szasz, *The Manufacture of Madness*, 238.

9. William E. Davis, *The Special Educator: Strategies for Succeeding in Today's Schools* (Austin: Pro-Ed, 1983), 139.

10. See Nancy A. Madden and Robert E. Slavin, *Count Me In: Academic Achievement and Social Outcomes of Mainstreaming Students with Mild Academic Handicaps*, Report No. 329, Center for Social Organization of Schools, The Johns Hopkins University, 1982.

9 **Learning Disabilities**

1. Laurence Lieberman, *Preventing Special Education . . . for Those Who Don't Need It* (Weston, Mass.: Nobb Hill Press, 1984), 81.

2. James E. Ysseldyke and Bob Algozzine, "LD or Not LD: That's Not the Question," *Journal of Learning Disabilities* 16 (January 1983):29–32.

3. Diane McGuinness, *When Children Don't Learn: Understanding the Biology and Psychology of Learning Disabilities* (New York: Basic Books, 1985), 19.

4. See Gerald S. Coles, C.M.D.N.J., Rutgers Medical School, "The Learning Disability Test Battery: Empirical and Social Issues," *Harvard Education Review* 48 (August 1978):313–40. He writes on page 323: "To date, research shows that neurologists are no closer than learning-disabilities specialists to establishing a relationship between minimal neurological dysfunction and learning problems."

5. Dr. Frank H. Mayfield, a neurosurgeon and educator, quoted in Ragene B. Pernecke and Sara M. Schreiner, *Schooling*

for the Learning Disabled: A Selective Guide to LD Programs in Elementary and Secondary Schools Throughout the United States (Chicago: SMS Publishing Corp., 1983), 34.

6. Harold B. Levy, M.D., *Square Pegs Round Holes: the Learning Disabled Child in the Classroom and at Home* (Boston: Little, Brown, 1973), 145.

7. Levy writes on page 204: "The response that the child makes to medication, lengthening of attention span, reduction of distractibility, improvement of the emotional control, and better concentration, I consider the most important evidence of the fact that he does indeed have an inherent biochemical disorder." For a comprehensive discussion of the medical controversy over drug use with learning-disabled children, see Peter Schrag and Diane Divoky, *The Myth of the Hyperactive Child* (New York: Pantheon Books, 1975), 76–89.

8. McGuinness, *When Children Don't Learn*, 172.

9. R. C. Lewontin, Steven Rose, and Leon J. Kamin, *Not in Our Genes, Biology, Ideology, and Human Nature* (New York: Pantheon Books, 1984), 192–93.

10. McGuinness, *When Children Don't Learn*, 175.

11. Dr. Melvin Levine, Chief of the Division of Ambulatory Pediatrics at The Children's Hospital, Boston, "Learning: Abilities and Disabilities," *Harvard Medical School Health Letter*, September 1984, 3.

12. Sandra Blakeslee, "Brain Studies Shed Light on Disorders," *New York Times Education Fall Survey*, 11 November 1984.

13. James Tucker, Linda J. Stevens, James E. Ysseldyke, "Learning Disabilities: The Experts Speak Out," *Journal of Learning Disabilities* 16 (January 1983):10.

14. *The School-Age Handicapped*, Contractor Report, National Center for Education Statistics, Child Trends Inc., prepared for U.S. Dept. of Education (Washington, D.C.: GPO, 1985), 67.

15. Dr. Doris Johnson, Dr. Lyndel Bullock, Dr. Laura Johnson, Howard Atlas, and Dr. Cindy Terry, *LD or Not?*, Illinois State Board of Education pamphlet, July 1984, 1.

16. "The School-Age Handicapped," 67.

10   Not Special and Not Education

1. Nancy A. Madden and Robert E. Slavin, *Count Me In: Academic Achievement and Social Outcomes of Mainstreaming with Mild*

Academic Handicaps, Report No. 329, Center for Social Organization of Schools, The Johns Hopkins University, 1982, 1.

2. Ibid., 59

3. Ibid., 60

4. Daniel P. Hallahan and James M. Kauffman, *Exceptional Children: Introduction to Special Education* (Englewood Cliffs, N.J.: Prentice-Hall, 1982), 435.

5. James E. Ysseldyke, Ph.D., "Current Practices in Making Psychoeducational Decisions About Learning Disabled Students," *Journal of Learning Disabilities* 16 (April 1983):229.

6. *The School-Age Handicapped,* Contractor Report, National Center for Education Statistics, Child Trends Inc., prepared for U.S. Dept. of Education (Washington, D.C.: GPO, 1985), 20.

7. Harry N. Chandler, M.Ed., "You Can't Call It Failure: Elementary LD Education," *Journal of Learning Disabilities* 15 (January 1982):503–4.

8. Ysseldyke, "Current Practices," 230.

9. David Melton, *When Children Need Help* (New York: Thomas Y. Crowell, 1972), 121.

10. Ibid.

11. Harold M. Murai, Ph.D., "Eligibility Criteria for Learning Disability Programs: Institutionalized Discrimination," *Journal of Learning Disabilities* 15 (May 1982):267.

12. Gerald S. Coles, C.M.D.N.J., Rutgers Medical School, "The Learning Disability Test Battery: Empirical and Social Issues," *Harvard Education Review* 48 (August 1978):334.

13. Quoted in James E. Ysseldyke and Bob Algozzine, "LD or Not LD: That's Not the Question," *Journal of Learning Disabilities* 16 (January 1983):29.

11   **Breaking Through the Special Ed Jargon Jungle**

1. Diane McGuinness, *When Children Don't Learn: Understanding the Biology and Psychology of Learning Disabilities* (New York: Basic Books, 1985), 46.

2. Lieberman, *Preventing Special Education . . . for Those Who Don't Need It* (Weston, Mass.: Nob Hill Press, 1984), 86.

3. *The School-Age Handicapped,* Contractor Report, National Center for Education Statistics, Child Trends Inc., prepared for U.S. Dept. of Education (Washington, D.C.: GPO, 1985), 63.

4. McGuinness, *When Children Don't Learn,* 168.

13   **The New Segregation**

1. Larry Maheady, Bob Algozzine, and James Ysseldyke, "Minorities in Special Education," *The Education Digest* 51 (December 1985):50.

2. Ibid.

3. *The School-Age Handicapped,* Contractor Report, National Center for Education Statistics, Child Trends Inc., prepared for U.S. Dept. of Education (Washington, D.C.: GPO, 1985), 29.

4. Maheady, Algozzine, and Ysseldyke, "Minorities," 50.

5. See, for example, Marleen C. Pugach, *The Limitations of Federal Special Education Policy: The Role of Classroom Teachers in Determining Who Is Handicapped,* Ph.D. dissertation, University of Illinois, Urbana, reprinted in *Journal of Special Education* 19 (Spring 1985):123–34. She writes on page 124: "The teacher's original description of the referred student substantially influences subsequent descriptions made by other support services personnel responsible for conducting impartial evaluations; studies of decision making indicate that such initial impressions have a tendency to persist even in the face of new data which question its accuracy."

6. Designs for Change, *Caught in the Web: Misplaced Children in Chicago's Classes for the Mentally Retarded*, December 1982, 17.

7. Marva Collins and Civia Tamarkin, *Marva Collins' Way* (Los Angeles: J.P. Tarcher, 1982), 112.

8. Northwestern University study, reported in "Black Pupils Chalk Up Success in Suburbs," *Chicago Tribune*, 18 December 1985.

9. Harry N. Chandler, M.Ed., and Karen Jones, M.Ed., "Learning Disabled or Emotionally Disturbed: Does It Make Any Difference?" *Journal of Learning Disabilities* 17 (August/September 1983):432–34.

10. Robert B. Edgerton, *Mental Retardation* (Cambridge: Harvard University Press, 1979), 3–4.

11. Ibid.

12. Gerald S. Coles, C.M.D.N.J., Rutgers Medical School, "The Learning Disability Test Battery: Empirical and Social Issues," *Harvard Education Review* 48 (August 1978):333.

13. Walter Lippmann, "The Reliability of Intelligence Tests," *The New Republic*, 1922, reprinted in *The I.Q. Controversy*,

ed. N.J. Block and Gerald Dworkin (New York: Random House, 1976), 17.

14   How to Save Your Child

1. Jerome Rosner, *Helping Children Overcome Learning Difficulties: A Step-by-Step Guide for Parents and Teachers* (New York: Walker, 1979), 61.

2. Rudolf Dreikurs, M.D., *Psychology in the Classroom, A Manual for Teachers* (New York: Harper & Row, 1968), 10.

3. Annual meeting panel reported in *Illinois School Board Journal* 52 (January/February 1984):57.

4. James E. Ysseldyke, Ph.D., "Current Practices in Making Psychoeducational Decisions About Learning Disabled Students," *Journal of Learning Disabilities* 16 (April 1983):228.

5. Harry N. Chandler, M.Ed., "Mainstreaming: A Formative Consideration," *Journal of Learning Disabilities* 19 (February 1986):499.

6. Gerald S. Coles, C.M.D.N.J., Rutgers Medical School, "The Learning Disability Test Battery: Empirical and Social Issues," *Harvard Education Review* 48 (August 1978):335.

16   Parents Are Teachers Too

1. Jerome Rosner, *Helping Children Overcome Learning Difficulties: A Step-by-Step Guide for Parents and Teachers* (New York: Walker, 1979), 153–54.

2. Ibid., 153.

3. Marva Collins and Civia Tamarkin, *Marva Collins' Way* (Los Angeles: J. P. Tarcher, 1982), 110–11.

17   Making Schools Work

1. Toni Ginnetti, "Still Outspoken, Dr. Spock Puts Pediatrics Over Politics," *Chicago Sun-Times*, 11 January 1983.

2. Ibid.

3. Quoted in Rudolf Flesch, *Why Johnny STILL Can't Read* (New York: Harper & Row, 1981), 130.

19   Seeing and Hearing

1. Norman Geschwind, quoted by Jean L. Marx in "Autoimmunity in Left-handers," *Science* 217 (9 July 1982):141–142.

2. Richard Anderson, *Becoming a Nation of Readers*, National Academy of Education Commission on Reading, 1985.

3. Ralph Nader, comments to a conference of the Optometric Extension Program, 1980.

4. A. M. Skeffington, "The Analytical Examination: A Dynamic Concept of Vision," undated tape-recording supplied by the Optometric Extension Program, 1960.

5. Richard S. Kavner, *Your Child's Vision* (New York: Simon and Schuster, 1985), 207–208.

6. Ibid., 208.

Recommended Books

Baron, Bruce, Christine Baron, and Bonnie MacDonald. *What Did You Learn in School Today?* New York: Warner Books, 1975.

A useful checklist for parents interested in knowing just where their child should be according to the public school curriculum. It can be an eye-opening book; some parents have told us that they discovered that children they were assured were hopelessly behind class standards were actually well ahead! It is also a useful way to find out where your child's class stands as compared to others in the country. Written by public school teachers, the book provides some simple reading tests and helpful hints on teaching mathematics. It also presents the standard educators' line on Special Education; this can be safely ignored.

Bettelheim, Bruno, and Karen Zelan. *On Learning to Read: The Child's Fascination with Meaning,* New York: Alfred A. Knopf, 1981.

Yet another book that critiques the way reading is taught in this country, but from a novel point of view. Bettelheim and Zela think the "dumbing down" of textbooks and reading materials in schools is the result of a lack of respect for children and what they can learn and want to learn. They see children as eager to make sense of the world and to join the adult community, unlike the picture of them that is common in public schools as passive, uninterested, play-oriented beings.

Collins, Marva, and Civia Tamarkin. *Marva Collins' Way*. Los Angeles: J.P. Tarcher, 1982.

The story of one tough and opinionated teacher's struggle to set up a school that would give an opportunity for success to children written off as losers on Chicago's black West Side. Marva Collins' philosophy of teaching is based on the idea that teachers must really teach, and they must not allow their students to fail. As she struggles with the reality of her students' past failures and current problems, her story can be both shocking and depressing, but it tells of ultimate success.

Feuerstein, Reuven. *Instrumental Enrichment*. Baltimore, Md.: University Park Press, 1979.

This technically written book by an Israeli psychologist is required reading for any parent who has had a child diagnosed as retarded. Feuerstein, who is in his eighties and has worked with troubled children since the end of World War II, is dead-set against the idea of IQ tests and the static idea of intelligence that they represent. He maintains that the basic need a child has in order to develop his intelligence is a "mediated learning experience," most often provided by his parents. If different factors—such as physical handicaps, poverty, or institutional care—have prevented his obtaining that experience at the usual age, Feuerstein has developed a system of teaching to develop his intelligence. Working with adolescents, Feuerstein appears to have had good success with children others had written off as too organically or emotionally damaged to learn. He argues against a "passive acceptant" attitude toward children with test scores in the retarded range and views them as having untapped potential.

Flesch, Rudolf. *Why Johnny Can't Read—and What You Can Do About It*. New York: Harper & Brothers, 1955.

Thirty years after it appeared, this remains the best single book on what happened to excellence in American education. Along with a thorough critique of the kind of educational thinking that has led to near illiteracy for a large number of our youth, Flesch, a lawyer and education consultant who was raised in Austria, provides a step-by-step phonics program to help parents teach their children the basic reading skills they're still all too likely to miss in our schools.

Gould, Stephen Jay. *The Mismeasure of Man.* New York: W.W. Norton, 1981.

The natural historian and author of a number of popular books on science provides a thorough and scathing documentation of how we arrived at the idea that intelligence can be measured. Along the way he provides a fascinating account of wrongheaded ideas, prejudices, and simple blind spots among men who imagined themselves to be objective scientists. His discussion of the statistical methods often referred to in the social sciences is brilliant and readable.

Holt, John. *Teach Your Own.* New York: Delacorte, 1981.

A prominent sixties-style radical in education, Holt was a teacher who became convinced that schools in this country are so stifling for children that most would be better off learning at home. This book presents his experiences in helping parents to set up their own home-schooling programs.

Kavner, Richard, O.D. *Your Child's Vision: A Parent's Guide to Seeing, Growing, and Developing.* New York: Simon and Schuster, 1985.

Kavner has thoroughly considered the theory behind today's optometric treatments and why developmental optometrists believe that a large number of the children schools call retarded, learning-disabled, or emotionally disturbed in reality have vision problems. He discusses the major role of vision in child and personality development, and he talks about what should be done for a child with a developmental vision problem.

Lewontin, R. C., Steven Rose, and Leon J. Kamin. *Not in Our Genes: Biology, Ideology and Human Nature.* New York: Pantheon Books, 1984.

A book by a neurologist, a psychologist, and an evolutionary geneticist, this debunks many of the pretensions of psychometricians. The view that "science" can establish standards of human behavior and then provide techniques for changing people to fit those standards comes in for a great deal of erudite ridicule. Their section on drug use in schools is enlightening.

McGuinness, Diane. *When Children Don't Learn: Understanding the Biology and Psychology of Learning Disabilities.* New York: Basic Books, 1985.

McGuinness is a psychologist who has done extensive work in the area of male/female differences in learning. In this book she reviews the research work that underlies our assumptions about the children we call learning-disabled. The book contains important work on the question of how boys differ from girls in their development and how schools and researchers have tended to ignore the differences.

Rosner, Jerome. *Helping Children Overcome Learning Difficulties: A Step-by-Step Guide for Parents and Teachers.* New York: Walker, 1979.

Jerome Rosner is an optometrist who has worked with children, child-development researchers, and Special Educators for thirty years. His book gives a thorough consideration of auditory and visual-perceptual problems in children—how they can be identified and how they can be remediated. Along with these programs, however, he stresses that the child's academic weaknesses should be worked on simultaneously, and he gives step-by-step descriptions of techniques for teaching reading, mathematics facts, spelling, and handwriting to children having difficulty in these areas. Rosner's orientation is toward the practical, toward what works. His tone is reasonable and reassuring, and he has a thorough—and skeptical—knowledge of the development of the field of Special Education.

Schrag, Peter, and Diane Divoky. *The Myth of the Hyperactive Child.* New York: Pantheon Books, 1975.

A decade ago, a journalist and an education writer set out to document the growing use of drugs, therapy, and testing to control "deviant" children. Today their book has proven to be prophetic, since the abuses they cited have become even more accepted and the number of children subject to these questionable methods has roughly doubled. They discuss the history behind the use of drugs on schoolchildren, the abuse of school files on children, and the political implications of the trend toward identifying more and more children as learning-disabled or minimally brain-damaged.

Szasz, Thomas S., M.D. *The Manufacture of Madness.* New York: Harper & Row, 1970.

Szasz, a psychiatrist once described by *Time* magazine as "the ankle-biter at psychological conventions," writes a dry and witty prose on the absurdity of some of the pretensions of modern psychiatry. Any parent who finds himself caught up in the jargon and intimidation of school "psychoeducational evaluation" ought to read Szasz for another viewpoint on what is happening to him and his child.

Whimbey, Arthur with Linda Shaw Whimbey. *Intelligence Can Be Taught.* New York: E.P. Dutton, 1980.

An examination of the evidence behind the idea that what we call intelligence is actually a set of skills that can be taught in a systematic fashion, rather than something fixed at birth. The authors have investigated a number of approaches to increasing those skills, especially for disadvantaged preschoolers, and provide a comprehensive discussion of several successful programs.

Acknowledgments

This book grew reluctantly. It grew from our problem with the schools and our son. It grew from our necessary research. It grew from our rather terrible experiences. It grew and grew because we had to know more. But it wasn't intended to be a book. The knowledge we gained was to help us—three Grangers—and not to help others.

Along the way, we got unexpected and warm helping hands. Some came from teachers, some from others who had studied the problem, some from editors, some from researchers and those who knew the law. Gradually, the knowledge we had gained became columns in a important newspaper, then an article in the most widely read magazine in the country, and now it is a book.

This book is intended to help other parents who are faced with the same problems—and choices—we faced. You are not alone. We learned, in our struggle, that we were not alone, either. We would like to thank some of the people who helped us, encouraged us, stood up for us when we needed their support.

Thanks first to James B. Squires, the editor of the *Chicago Tribune*, and F. Richard Ciccone, the managing editor. When our struggle began, Ciccone was a friend and confidant, sharing his own experiences to help us see our way clear to solving our problems. He was more than an editor.

Both Squires and Ciccone made the lonely decision to publish the first articles on our experiences with Special Education. The pressure applied to these newspaper executives from education groups following publication was tremendous. They knew it would come—and they stuck to their decision to publish. Organized writing protests flooded their offices—and filled their telephone lines—with withering fire. They took the fire; they never backed down.

Norman Lewis Smith, a senior editor of *Reader's Digest*, urged us for a year to make our experiences known in an article for his magazine. We were reluctant; we had been caught in that first firestorm of protest from the education establishment. Smith persisted, and when the article was written, he piloted it through the layers of the editing process at that magazine. We are grateful to him as well.

Mrs. Jean Reed, a wise and experienced kindergarten teacher, who had wide experience in teaching "different" children, was one of the first to help us try to make sense of the Special Education nightmare. Dr. Daniel Nast, Jr., a developmental optometrist who solved our son's physical problems, volunteered his services out of the blue. Thanks too are due to Jan Puccio, the therapist who helped our son see.

We are also grateful for the advice on visual problems in children we received from Dr. Leonard Peiser. Special Educators James Early of the University of Indiana and Howard Blackman of the LaGrange (Illinois) Area Department of Special Education were generous of their time and talents in sharing ideas with us. Thanks also to a school board member, Sandra Stuart.

We are grateful for the help and encouragement we received from some very fine educators: Shirley Mallot, Barbara Creevy, Patricia Joy, Larry Lewis, Bernice Lynaugh, Estelle Desai, Mary Gerut, and Louise Mangos. Thanks to a private psychotherapist, Carol Schuham, who spoke of her specialty in frank and humanistic terms and shared her knowledge with us.

Thanks to Sheila Radford-Hill, whose organization has

struggled to support parents—particularly inner-city black parents whose children have been wrongly diagnosed into the Special Education trap. Patrick Murphy, public guardian of Cook County, Illinois, a good friend whose practice of law—in the public and private sector—has won rights for children without many rights, also helped us with advice and encouragement. In addition, attorney Russell Fee helped us research the maze of Special Education laws, and did it as a favor without expectation of reward.

Former State Representative Diana Nelson, herself a teacher, shared some constructive notions about education and the law and offered valuable assistance in our research.

Insofar as their ideas, philosophies, and sense of commitment are reflected in this book, they deserve the credit. If some of our conclusions are not shared by them—then it is because this book is, finally, our product, and the mistakes in it are our mistakes, and the conclusions reached are our conclusions. We have received skillful editorial direction from Richard Marek at Dutton, who has been careful to make sure this is *our* book, reflecting *our* ideas.

For several years, what we knew and what we said was disseminated more widely by two *Chicago Tribune* employees who gave "extra" concern to telling other parents about our experiences in Special Education. No one is paid enough to go through the extra work—and they did it with a volunteer spirit that made us grateful. Mary Ann Stenson and Erva Woodward are the colleagues who got the word out to all the hundreds and thousands who telephoned or wrote to the *Tribune* to get information on our problem—and theirs.

We cannot adequately thank the literally thousands of parents and educators who have contacted us over the past three years to share their own stories. We have talked to many of them about their experiences, brainstormed with others about what it all means, and we have picked up useful hints and teaching strategies from still others.

Because these thousands took the time to share their stories, the need for this book grew in our minds and in the minds of others. This little note is not thanks enough. It was all these thousands who impelled us to write this book. We hope we have done a small amount of justice to show our thanks.

Index

Ritalin, 93, 94, 95, 125
Rorschach test, 74–75, 78
Rose, Steven, 246–47
Rosner, Jerome, 164, 184, 185,
    187, 188, 222, 247
Rushakoff, Laura, 43

Schooling for the Learning Disabled:
    a Selective Guide to LD
    Programs in Elementary and
    Secondary Schools Throughout
    the United States, 93
Schrag, Peter, 247–48
Schultz, Karen, 43
Scriven, Michael, 111–12
Seals, Ted, 43
Segregation of Special Education
    students, xi, 16–17, 52, 53,
    83, 108, 109, 126–27
  in full-time programs, 102,
    103, 105
  minority students, 146,
    150–51, 152–53
  negative effects of, 103, 104,
    106, 111, 122, 124
  see also Racial uses of Special
    Education
Seguin (French doctor), 209
"Sensory integration," exercises
    to improve, 97
Sex differences, 181
  hyperactivity, 125
  on IQ test scores, 90
  learning disability, 89–90, 91
  in learning language skills, 90,
    117, 216, 217
  in maturity, 116–17
Shockley, Dr. Alvin, 58
Siblings, 140
Signing consent forms, 5, 6, 9,
    19–20, 33, 114, 127, 129,
    167
Skeffington, A. M., 226–27
Social workers, 57, 58, 59, 138,
    152
Soft neurological damage, 131
Spearman, Charles, 64
Speech impairments, children
    with, 109

Alec's problem, 12–13, 18, 19,
    23, 41–42, 80
Speech therapy, 116
Spina bifida, 102
Spock, Benjamin, 193–94
Squires, James B., 39, 40
Stanford-Binet test, 68
State University of New York
    (Syracuse), 76
Statistics on Special Education,
    52–53, 58
  on children identified as
    needing help, xi, 8, 73–74,
    87, 89, 98–99
  on children in Special
    Education, xii, 8, 44, 53,
    90–91, 124, 148, 152–53,
    163
  on drug treatment, 94
  on hyperactivity, 125
  on mainstreaming, 108
  on success rates, 104–105
Sterilization of black girls, 67
Stern, W., 62
Strabismus (crossed eyes), 224,
    226, 227–28
Stutterers, 150
Szasz, Dr. Thomas, 76–78, 80,
    234, 248

Tamarkin, Civia, 188, 245
Tax credits, 214, 215
Teachers, 57–58, 63, 111, 198
  identifying children needing
    Special Education, x, xi, 8,
    11, 33, 54–55, 74, 81–82,
    91, 98, 99, 115, 141,
    149–50, 151
  IQ testing and labeling of
    children by, 69–70, 71–72
  letters of complaint from,
    165–67, 174
  parents as, see Home education
  principles of good teaching,
    207–208
  racial prejudice among, 146,
    147, 149–50, 152
  Special Education, 26, 43,
    52–53, 55, 82–83, 103, 105,

ABOUT THE AUTHORS

LORI GRANGER grew up in Chicago and Washington, D.C. She received a B.A. degree from Antioch College (Yellow Springs, Ohio). She received her M.A. degree, specializing in inner-city political science, from Roosevelt University, Chicago. She studied as a fellow of the National Opinion Research Center, Chicago, and as a doctoral candidate in political science at the University of Chicago. She was an editor at the Day Newspapers in suburban Chicago and operated her own news syndicate—Central News of Chicago—reporting on political matters in the city and state. She has contributed to *The Reader* newspaper, the *Illinois Issues* political magazine, and other publications.

She has taught political science at the Illinois Institute of Technology and DePaul University. She has also worked as an editor, producing a series of readers for children in elementary school, at Follet Publishing Company. She was also an editor of the educational-services division of the *Encyclopaedia Britannica*. With her husband, she is co-author of *Fighting Jane*, a study of Mayor Jane Byrne of Chicago, published by Dial Press.

BILL GRANGER was born and raised in Chicago. He went to DeLaSalle Institute in Chicago and DePaul University, where he majored in English. He was named to *Who's Who in American Colleges and Universities* while at college. His first newspaper job was as a copyboy at the *Chicago Daily News*. He left college in his senior year to work for United Press International. He worked for the *Chicago Tribune* for two years in the 1960s, worked for the *Chicago Sun-Times*, and has, since 1980, written a column for the *Chicago Tribune*. He has published sixteen novels. One of his novels won the Mystery Writers of America award, the Edgar, in 1980. He has reported from Chicago, across the United States, and in Europe. He has contributed to *The New Republic, Reader's Digest, Columbia Journalism Review, Time* magazine, *The New York Times*, the *Washington Post, Newsday*, and other journals. He taught, as a part-time vocation, writing and criticism at Columbia College, Chicago. He is listed in *Who's Who in America*.

ALEC GRANGER is ten. He plays the piano, skis, can touch-type, reads books, eats apples, has been to Paris, and loves Ginny Olmstead.